Sew Young, Sew Fun

Sew It Up!

Sew Young, Sew Fun

Sew It Up!

Viking Sewing Machines Inc. / Sewing Information Resources
Westlake, Ohio   St. Charles, IL

A HUSQVARNA VIKING / SIR KEEPING THE WORLD SEWING BOOK

SEWING INFORMATION RESOURCES
President: JoAnn Pugh-Gannon

VIKING SEWING MACHINES INC.
Senior Vice President Sales and Marketing: Stan Ingraham
Publicity Director: Nancy Jewell
Sew Young, Sew Fun host: Nina Kay Milenius

SEW IT UP! was produced in conjunction with:
Graphic Design: Ernie Shelton, Shelton Design Studios
Photography: Kaz Ayukawa, K Graphics
Sample making: Karen Kunkel, Gretchen McGinnis
Illustrations: phoenix advertising art
Index: Mary Helen Schiltz

Printed in China

ISBN 1-886884-11-0

Table

of Contents

Important Stuff!

A Note for You and a Grown-up
(page 8)

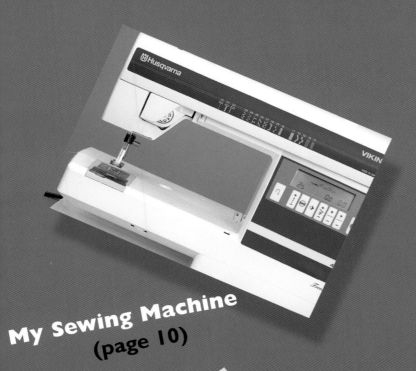

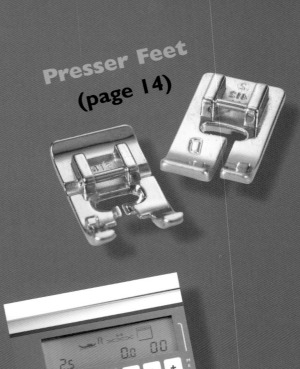

Important

A Note for You and A Grown-up

To be a good sewer:

1. Work with adult supervision. When sewing, you are working with lots of different types of equipment. It is important to get permission to cut, sew, print, or iron, first. If you have a special sewing and craft area or room at home, you are lucky, but most of you will need to work on the kitchen or dining room table. Remember to always ask first!

2. Learn all you can about your sewing machine. Read the instruction manual and take lessons from the local sewing machine dealer. The more you know, the smarter you sew!

3. Read and follow the directions. We recommend that you read the directions thoroughly that come with any pattern before you begin sewing. If you are using a pattern you bought at the store, you may be able to figure out another method of sewing a section because of what you have learned about your machine or a particular presser foot. Don't be afriad to try a new technique on your project!

Stuff!

4. Follow safety precautions with all your tools. The machine and iron use electricity; the iron gets hot; scissors, pins and the needle are sharp; and a rotary cutter can cut, too. Be respectful of your tools; treat them with care. The ruler shown here has a finger guard that helps you hold the ruler and avoid accidentally cutting yourself!

5. Clean up when you are done. Store your supplies in a safe place once you are finished away from helpful little sisters and brothers. Find a big basket or clear box with a lid to hold your sewing tools and notions. Or make yourself a handy sewing caddy as your next project!

6. So...Be you, be one of a kind, and Sew It Up! You did it yourself!

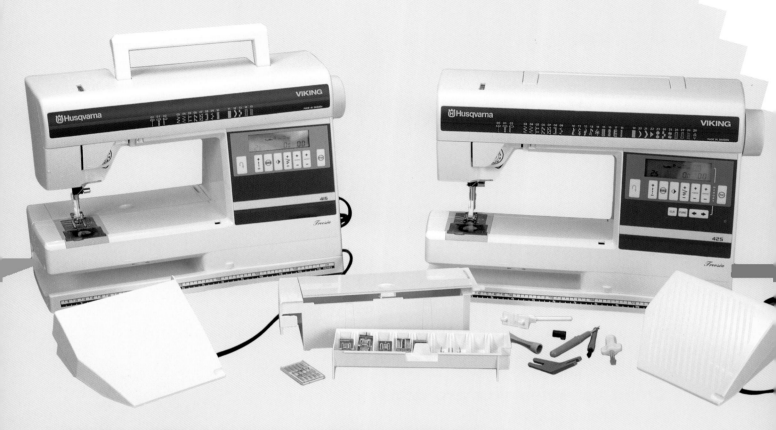

My Sewing Machine

The most important piece of equipment you will need when beginning to sew is your sewing machine. It can be your friend or your foe depending on how you treat it and how it treats you!

First, make sure the machine is cleaned and in good running order. If your machine is an older model and has not been used for a long time, take it to a sewing machine dealer for a good cleaning and tune-up. If the machine is in good condition when you begin, you are starting off on the right foot for learning to sew.

Second, the more you can learn about your machine the more fun you will have sewing. You may be able to take classes on your own machine at a sewing machine dealer's store. Learn what all the stitches can do and how to use all the presser feet. Read the instruction manual and the information here. We have also included a video section describing the parts of the sewing machine and how a stitch is formed, plus, lots more information on the CD.

The more you know...the smarter you sew!

Machine Functions

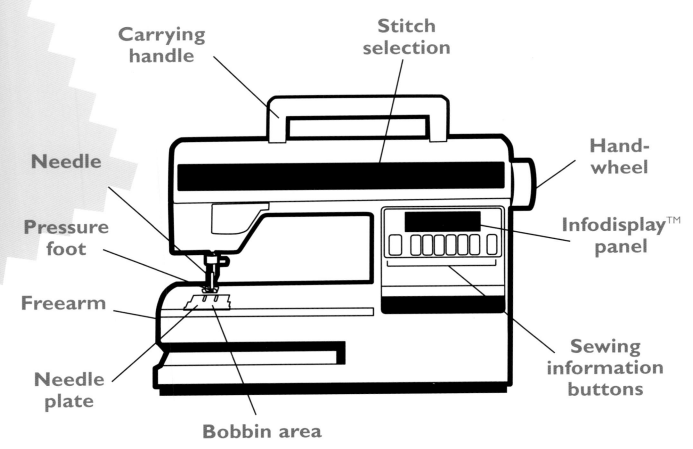

Carrying handle

Stitch selection

Needle

Hand-wheel

Pressure foot

Infodisplay™ panel

Freearm

Needle plate

Sewing information buttons

Bobbin area

Most sewing machines have the following functions visible on the front of the machine, right at your fingertips. Be sure to read your instruction manual to locate all these important features.

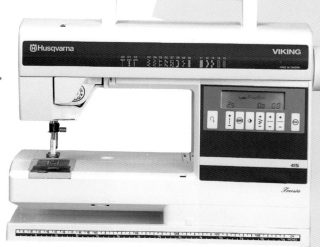

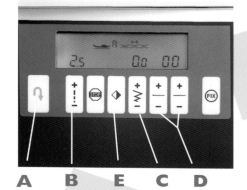

A   B   E   C   D

Reverse (A)

Press this button or one similar, continuously, to sew backwards. When the button is released, the machine sews forward. Some machines have another button for constant reverse. Check your sewing machine manual for more information.

Stitch Length (B)

Most computerized sewing machines will automatically set the best stitch length when a specific stitch is selected. Use the stitch length button to adjust the length for the fabric or technique you are sewing.

Stitch Width (C)

As with the stitch length, a computerized sewing machine will automatically select the best stitch width for you when the stitch is selected. Change the width by pressing the button, plus or minus, for your fabric or technique. This button may also adjust your needle position when you are using a selected straight stitch. The **Mirror Image** function **(E)** will move the needle to the other side.

Stitch Selection Button (D)

Use this button or buttons to choose the appropriate stitch for the project you are sewing. Some machines have one button per stitch while others may have a visible display like you see here with digitally displayed numbers for each stitch.

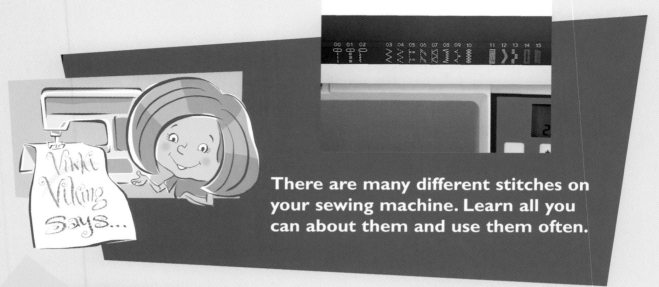

There are many different stitches on your sewing machine. Learn all you can about them and use them often.

Thread Tension

Most computerized sewing machines automatically adjust the thread tension for the stitch you are using. Some machines allow you to fine-tune this function by letting you select the type and weight of fabric you are sewing on first. This function can easily be adjusted either manually with a dial or by using a button—plus or minus.

Special Machine Functions and Features

There are many other machine functions that may come with your machine. The more you know about your machine the easier your sewing projects will be. Read the manual and take advantage of any sewing machine classes the local dealer may offer.

Fix—Many sewing machines can lock the threads at the beginning and end of the stitch using this type of function. **Mirror Image**—This function allows you to flip the stitch to the other side mirroring the design exactly. **Memory**—This function allows your machine to memorize a stitch or sequence of stitches. Some machines have multiple memory banks. **Clear**—This button is used most often to delete what you have programmed into your machine. Check your machine manual for the complete use of the clear button.
Presser Foot Display—Many machines indicate visually on the LCD screen the correct foot to use for the stitch chosen.

Presser Feet

Each sewing machine comes with a group of basic presser feet that correspond to the functions on your machine. The more you know about your machine and how to use each foot, the easier your sewing will be. The presser feet for your machine may be identified by either a letter or number. Learn what function each foot performs by the letter as well as by sight.

All-purpose Foot

This foot is used for most normal straight sewing. The needle hole will accommodate any needle position for topstitching.

Decorative Foot

This foot is used for most zig zag and satin-stitch-type stitches. The bottom of the foot is cut away to let the stitches pass under the foot easily. The needle hole will accommodate any needle position.

Buttonhole Foot

This special foot works with the style of buttonholes on your machine. Read your instruction manual carefully to understand how your buttonholes are sewn. Find out if your buttonhole system is fully automatic and remembers the buttonhole size for repetitive same-size buttonholes, or semi-automatic where you must press the reverse button to change the direction of the sewing. Always sew out a buttonhole first on a scrap of your project fabric before sewing on your project.

Zipper Foot

This foot is designed to fit up close to the zipper teeth on both sides of the needle. Either snap the foot to the left or right of the needle or move the needle position before sewing.

Blindhem Foot

This special foot is designed to guide the fold of the fabric during stitching. Also use this foot for edge stitching if you don't own an edge joining foot.

Overcast Foot

This foot is used to overcast the edges of many fabrics using the overcast stitches on your machine. The small pin on the side of the foot keeps finer fabrics from puckering and rolling while stitching.

There are many other extra presser feet that you will be introduced to throughout this book. They are each designed to help you perform a particular sewing job with ease. As you begin to sew more and more, you will want to purchase these feet to make your sewing quicker and easier.

Basic Sewing Supplies

There are a few basic sewing supplies besides your machine that you will need before getting started on your first sewing project. After you have read this section of the book and decided which project you want to sew, take a trip to the fabric store or your local sewing machine dealer to purchase your sewing supplies. Here are descriptions of some of the things you will need and you will find out more throughout this book. Also watch the video section on the CD for more information on your basic sewing "notions."

Needles

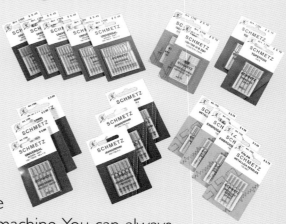

We can talk about needles when we talk about the sewing machine or when we talk about sewing supplies. As you can see from the picture here there are many different kinds and sizes of needles.

First, you need to choose the right size needle for the weight of the fabric you are sewing on. A standard-size needle for most sewing projects and the ones in this book would be an #80/12. Make sure you are buying the correct brand of needle for your machine. You can always ask the sales person or check your instruction manual if you have any questions.

There are also a number of special needles used for special projects. These embroidery and metallic needles, for example, are used if you are sewing with fine decorative or metallic threads. The needles help keep the thread from breaking or fraying during sewing. Check out all the different kinds of needles.

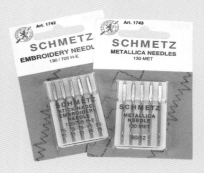

Thread

You will see many different kinds of thread in the store. For most of your sewing projects, you will need a good quality polyester sewing thread. This can be 100% polyester or a cotton-wrapped/polyester core thread. It is strong for your seams and is your basic sewing thread.

There are also special decorative threads made from rayon, silks, or other fiber combinations. These threads are used for machine embroidery or other decorative work.

Pins

You will have a lot of choices in the pin section too! As a beginner you might want to select pins with colored heads. They are easier to grasp with the larger head. And buy a magnetic pincushion to keep your pins together.

Pattern Tracing Material

You will be using pattern tracing material to trace off patterns found on the CD for many of the projects in this book. .You can buy 1" grided tracing material by the yard. Usually this notion is found in the interfacing section of the store.

Fabric Marking Pencils, Pens, and Chalk

There are many different types of marking tools for you to choose from. Read the packages carefully before you buy. Some pencils and pens will not come out after you have marked your fabric so be careful with your selection. Page 59 has more information about marking tools.

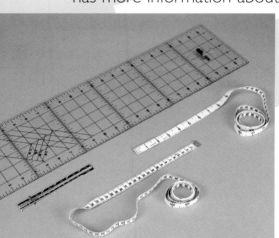

Measuring Tools

Purchase a long, clear plastic ruler; a seam gauge; and a tape measure to get started. You will find lots of uses for these measuring tools in all your projects. More about measuring tools are on page 58.

Scissors

A good pair of sewing scissors is a very important notion for sewing. Remember to keep these scissors separate from the ones you use to cut paper because the paper will dull the scissors. Pinking shears are also nice to own. Not only can you use the pinking shears to finish your seam allowances, but they also make a very decorative edge on exposed seams. See page 59 for more about pinking shears.

Iron

An iron is a necessity for sewing well. We believe in sewing a seam and then pressing as you go along. By pressing after stitching, you control the fabric better, eliminating the need to press the whole project at the end.

All About Fabrics

Let's learn a little bit about all the fabrics you will see in the fabric store. We've included a visit to a fabric store on the CD to make it easier for you to understand. There are so many fabrics to choose from that it can be confusing!

Cotton is a natural fiber made from the cotton plant. It is a woven fabric and comes in a variety of weights and widths. Cotton may be used for garments, quilting, and decorating projects. 100% cotton is washable, but it will shrink in hot water and wrinkles easily. So wash your fabric before you cut out the pattern. Cotton is very easy to sew with for a beginner.

Polyester is a man-made fiber that is made into a variety of fabric types. It may be soft, drape nicely, and have a silky feel, or it may look similar to cotton or wool. Polyester is used for garments and craft projects. It is washable, usually doesn't wrinkle, and is easy to care for.

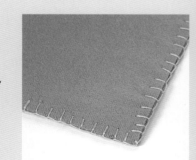

Wool is a natural fiber made from the wool sheared from sheep. It is available in a variety of weights, woven for coat weight called Melton to lightweight called challis. Wool is very durable and warm and is mainly used for garments. Most wool must be carefully hand-washed or dry cleaned, as it will shrink when washed in warm or hot water.

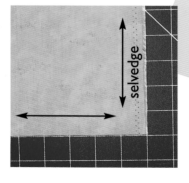

selvedge

Types of Fabric

Fabrics are generally divided into two types—woven or knit. Both types can be made from cotton, wool, polyester, or other man-made fibers.

Woven fabrics have threads that run in a lengthwise and crosswise direction at 90 degrees to each other. These

threads define the "grain" of the fabric. The selvedge will run the length of the fabric. The selvedge is the tightly woven edge of the fabric, which may give you information about the fabric like the fabric name or the manufacturer.
  The lengthwise grain will have very little stretch to it; the crosswise will have a small amount of stretch.

You may be asked to cut your fabric on the bias. This means to cut at a 45-degree angle. The fabric does stretch across the bias. Bias strips are used for bindings since the fabric can be stretched around curves.

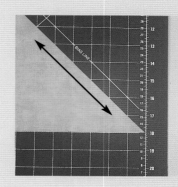

Knit fabrics may be made from polyester, cotton, or wool and are available in different weights. As the name describes, the fibers in these fabrics are knit together by machine rather than woven. One-way stretch knits stretch very little with the grain, but stretch a lot across the grain. Two-way stretch knits have equal stretch in both directions. Knits are used for sewing active wear and simple garments that require stretch and give with movement.

Sports fleece is a man-made, non-woven fabric with a soft cozy feel. It is perfect for bathrobes, jackets, sweatshirts, and simple blankets. It is fun and easy to work with since it does not fray and has no grainline. This fabric does have some stretch in the crosswise direction.

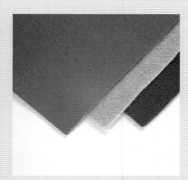

Felt is a non-woven, matted fabric made from wool or a combination of fibers that have been moistened and then pressed together. Felt does not ravel or fray and may be stiff from the dyes used to color it. Felt has no grain and is very easy to work with. It is a great fabric to use for craft projects and costumes.

I Want to Sew!

Sewing Exercises

The following sewing exercises will help you get started sewing! All of the exercise practice sheets are located on the CD for you to print and use. Print as many copies as you like. We will start sewing with the machine unthreaded so you can get used to controlling the sewing speed and the foot pedal. Practice the exercises over and over until you are comfortable with the main features of your own machine.

Just Sew You Know

Depending on the type of machine you are sewing on, you may have to select the stitch length and stitch width every time you change your stitch. Some machines automatically adjust to a predetermined stitch length and stitch width for each stitch, but you can still change them for the fabric you are sewing on.

Let's start with straight stitching! For this exercise print the exercise sheet marked "Straight and Zig Zag Stitching" on the CD.

First, turn the handwheel to raise the needle. Raise the sewing machine presser foot and place the paper under the needle. Turn the handwheel and lower the needle into the spot on the paper marked *Start*. Lower the presser

Sew!

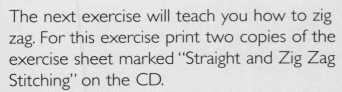

foot and slowly stitch the entire line. Stop when you reach the end of the line. Raise the needle and presser foot and remove the paper. Practice straight stitching on each line.
Change the stitch length if you want for each line!

The next exercise will teach you how to zig zag. For this exercise print two copies of the exercise sheet marked "Straight and Zig Zag Stitching" on the CD.

Set your sewing machine to a zig zag stitch (check the instruction manual for the correct number). Turn the handwheel to raise the needle. Lift the presser foot and place the lined paper under the needle. Turn the handwheel and lower the needle into the spot marked *Start*. Lower the presser foot and slowly stitch the entire line. Stop when you reach the end of the line. Raise the needle and presser foot and remove the paper. Practice stitching on each line with a different width zig zag stitch. Try this exercise again and change the stitch length too!

Continued

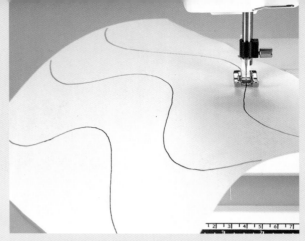

Sewing curves is the next exercise. Print the exercise sheet marked "Sewing Curves" on the CD.

Set your sewing machine to a straight stitch. Turn the handwheel and raise the needle. Lift the presser foot and place the curved-lined paper under the needle. Turn the handwheel to lower the needle into the spot on the paper marked *Start*. Lower the presser foot and begin stitching slowly turning the paper as you reach the curves. Stop when you reach the end of the line and remove the paper. Practice stitching the curves on each line. This exercise requires you to really control your speed!

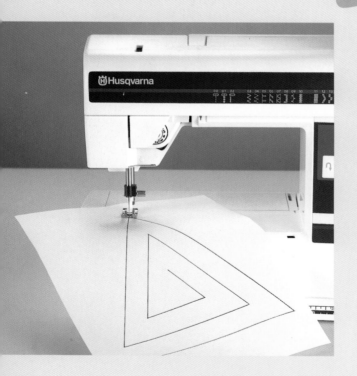

Turning corners is also an important sewing exercise to learn! Print the exercise sheet marked "Pivoting Corners" on the CD.

Set your sewing machine to a straight stitch. Turn the handwheel and raise the needle. Lift the presser foot and place the needle in the spot marked *Start* in the center of the triangle. Lower the presser foot and slowly stitch to the first corner. At the corner, leave the needle down in the paper and lift the presser foot. Turn the paper so the next line is centered under the foot. Lower the presser foot and continue sewing, turning and centering the paper at each corner.

Important Sewing Terms and Techniques

There are some very important sewing terms that you need to learn to begin your sewing projects. You will encounter different techniques and terms as you learn more and more about new fabrics, stitches, and patterns. If you learn good sewing habits, they will carry you through many, many exciting sewing projects. You will find many of these techniques on video on the **CD** that comes with this book. Read the information here first and then review the techniques shown on the **CD**. Have fun learning to sew!

Pinning

To pin your pattern pieces to the fabric, place the straight pins inside the pattern area and parallel to the edge of the pattern piece. Cut along the edges of the pattern piece through both layers of fabric.

Before sewing a seam, place two fabric pieces, right sides together, and pin the layers every 2" to 3" with the pins perpendicular to the cut edge of the fabric. You will be able to remove the pins easily once you start to sew.

Continued

Marking a Seam

To mark the stitching line, measure in $5/8$" from the edge of your fabric piece using your seam gauge and a fabric marking pen.

The standard seam allowance for sewing clothes is $5/8$" wide. The seam allowance for patchwork is $1/4$" and for home decorating sewing is $1/2$".

Just Sew You Know

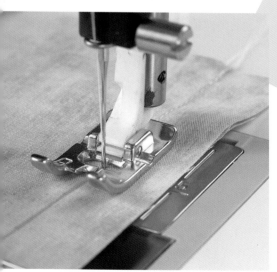

Sewing a Seam

To sew a $5/8$" seam, lift the presser foot and needle. Place the fabric under the foot with the edge even with the $5/8$" line on the needle plate. Turn the handwheel and place the needle in the stitching line about $1/2$" from the end of the fabric. To secure the end of the seam, backstitch to the end of the fabric and then sew along your seam line using your marked line and the throat plate as guides. At the end of the seam, backstitch again then raise the needle and presser foot, and remove the fabric. Cut the threads on the thread cutter.

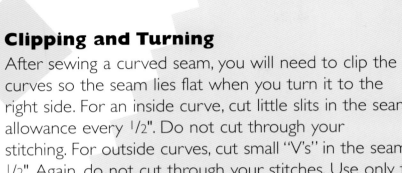

Clipping and Turning

After sewing a curved seam, you will need to clip the curves so the seam lies flat when you turn it to the right side. For an inside curve, cut little slits in the seam allowance every $1/2$". Do not cut through your stitching. For outside curves, cut small "V's" in the seam allowance about every $1/2$". Again, do not cut through your stitches. Use only the point of your scissors when clipping curves.

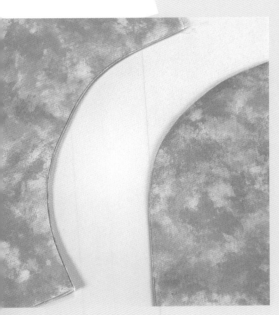

Once you have clipped your seams, turn your seams right side out and press. Be sure the stitching line is brought out to the edge of the fabric as you press.

Pressing Seams

To press open a seam, place your fabric right side down on your ironing board. Open the seam allowance and carefully press with the tip of your iron.

Versatile Shoulder Tote

Big or small, an easy drawstring bag can serve many purposes. A handy sports bag from canvas, a simple cotton laundry bag, or a larger overnight bag is a great starter project in sewing. Have fun decorating your bag anyway you want!

Gather your supplies:

- $^1/_2$ yard of fabric for small tote; $^3/_4$ yard of fabric for medium tote; 1 yard of fabric for large tote
- 1 yard of cotton webbing
- 1 yard of cording
- Pattern tracing material
- Fabric marking pencil, pen, or chalk
- Tape measure
- Polyester sewing thread
- Sewing scissors
- Pins
- Stamp and stamp pad or paint
- Letter template, paint, and brush

Sew for Yourself

Let's get started!

If you want to make a larger or smaller bag than given here, trace a circle for the desired size on pattern tracing material.

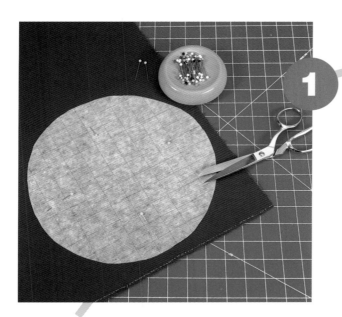

1 Copy the circle and rectangle patterns from the CD. Select from the small, medium, or large size bag. Refer to page 56 and tape the pieces together following the diagram. Trace the patterns onto pattern tracing material. Cut one circle and one rectangle from your fabric.

2

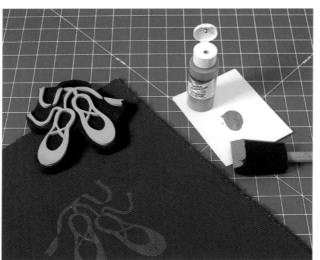

Decorate your bag with fun paints and stamps before you sew the pieces together. Randomly stamp the designs on the rectangle piece of fabric. Allow the paint to dry before sewing.

Continued

3

Using the stencil, paint, and brush or sponge, stencil your name on the strap as shown here.

Clean-finish one long edge of the rectangle with a serger or a zig zag stitch. Finish the side edges in the same manner. Press under 4" along this edge. Watch the video to learn more about the serger.

4

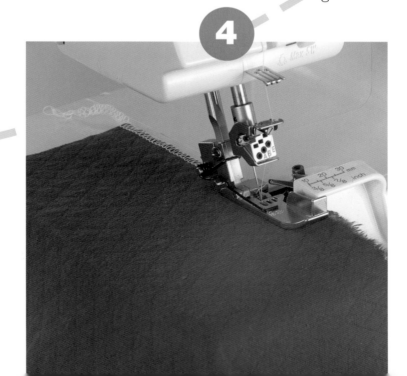

With fabric chalk and a tape measure, find the center of the top and bottom of the rectangle and mark for the strap placement.

5

6

On each short side of the rectangle, measure 6" down from the upper edge and mark using fabric chalk; measure down 1" from that mark and mark again to make an opening for the drawstring.

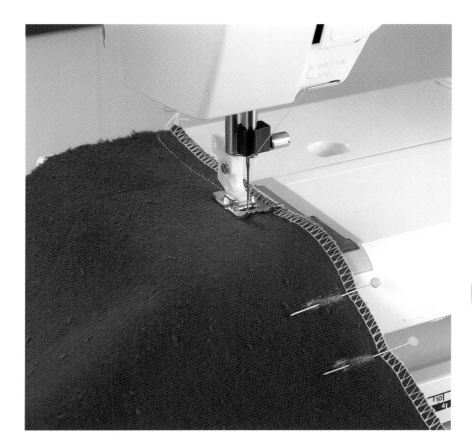

7

Match the short sides, right sides together, and stitch using a ¹/₂" seam allowance, leaving the seam open between the marks. Press the seam open.

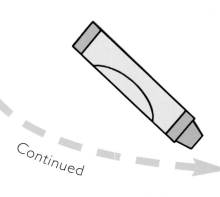

Continued

8

Pin the strap to the lower edge at the center mark. Using a very long stitch length, baste the end of the strap to the lower edge. Pin the bottom circle to the rectangle and stitch using a $1/2$" seam allowance. Serge-finish or zig-zag the seam edge.

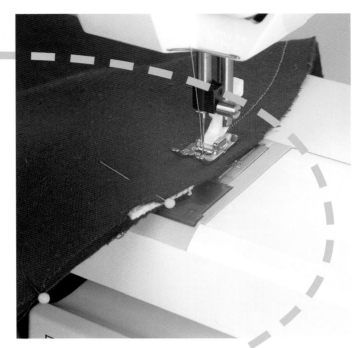

9

Place the other end of the strap at the center mark at the upper edge; baste in place. To form a drawstring casing, fold along the pressed line (step 5) and stitch close to the clean-finished edge.

On the right side of the fabric, measure down $1 1/2$" from the pressed edge and mark with a ruler and fabric chalk. Stitch along the mark to form the casing.

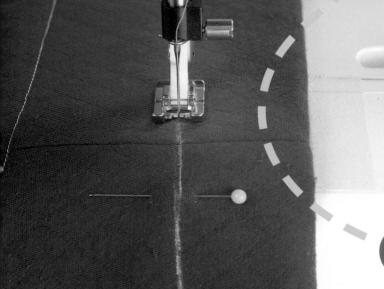

10

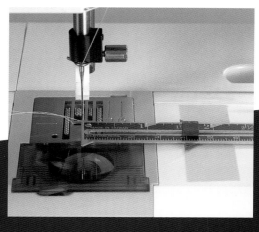

Vikki Viking Says...

To keep your stitching straight, make an easy guide for yourself. Measure from the needle 1 1/2" out and put a piece of masking tape on the bed of your machine. Guide the fabric edge along the masking tape edge for straight stitching.

11

To reinforce the strap at the top and bottom, stitch the strap to the side of the bag forming an "X" 1 1/2" long. Insert the cording through the opening at the side seam. And you are ready to go!

Easy Embroidered Bands

Make yourself one of these cool embroidered bands and wear it as a wristband, wrist key chain, or band for around your neck. Too cool!

Gather your supplies:

- 8"-long x 2"-wide piece of striped fabric such as cotton ticking for wristband; 10"-long X 1"-wide piece of fabric for wristband with hook; and 45"-long X 1"-wide piece of fabric for neckband
- Felt of same dimensions as striped fabric
- 3/4"-wide fusible webbing
- 5/8"-wide piece of Velcro® Sew-On hook and loop tape
- Polyester sewing thread
- #30-40 wt. rayon thread in assorted colors
- Iron
- Pins
- Rotating swivel hook
- Dual-feed foot (optional accessory)

Let's get started:

1

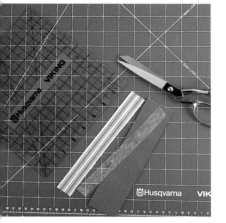

For a wristband, cut one piece of striped fabric 8" long x approximately 1" wide. Use the lines on the fabric to determine the exact width. Cut an 8" x 2" strip of felt.

2

Following the manufacturer's instructions, fuse the striped fabric to the center of the felt strip using the fusible webbing.

3

Attach the dual-feed foot, if available, and thread your machine with the rayon thread. Select a decorative stitch on your machine and stitch parallel rows using the stripes as your guide to keep the rows of stitches straight.

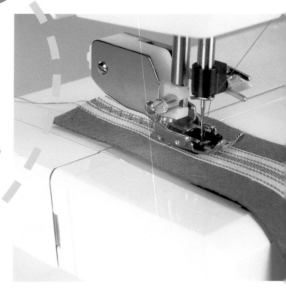

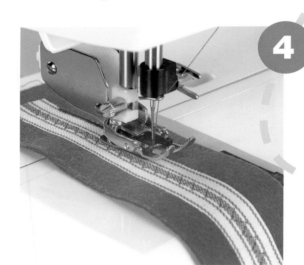

4

Finish the edges with a satin stitch. The dual-feed foot keeps the fabrics from sliding on each other.

Continued

A very tight zig zag stitch is called a satin stitch. Just shorten the length so the zig zags are close together without piling up on each other. Narrow your stitch width if the fabric starts to pucker or ripple.

Vikki Viking Says...

For the wrist key chain, cut one piece of striped fabric 10" long × 1" wide. Cut one piece of felt 10" long × 2" wide.

7

5 Trim the felt to ¹/4" along the long edges.

6

Sew the hook portion of the Velcro® Sew-On Tape to the right side of one end of the band with a straight stitch. Measure around your wrist and put a pin where the band is comfortable. Sew the loop portion to the back side of the band at the pin.

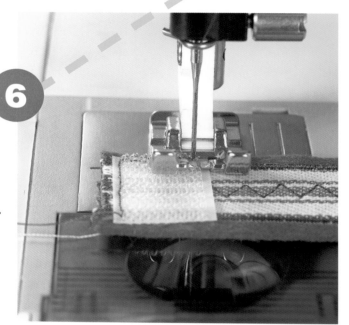

Vikki Viking says...

Check out the notions department at your local fabric store for hooks, buckles, buttons, or other fasteners you can use with your projects. They give your project that finishing touch!

8 Continue with steps 2 through 5 to decorate. Slide the swivel hook onto one end of the band and fold under 1". Stitch the end in place.

9 Follow step 6 for sewing the hook and loop tape to the band.

10 For the neckband, cut a piece of striped fabric 45" long × 1" wide and a felt piece 45" long × 2" wide .

11 Follow steps 2 through 5 for decorating the band.

Slide the swivel hook onto the band. Butt the cut ends together and sew the edges together with a very wide zig zag stitch. With wrong sides together, fold the neckband in half and measure up 3" from the hook. Satin-stitch through all thick-nesses, making sure to catch both edges in the stitching.

12

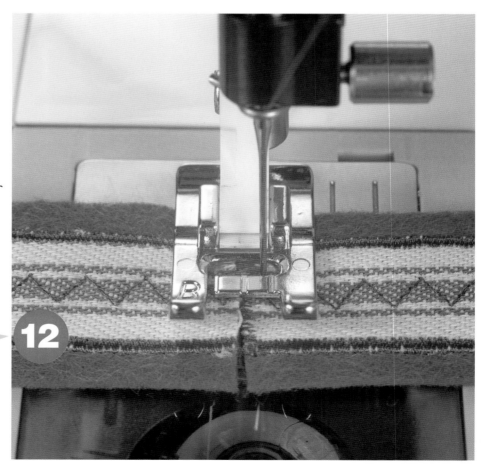

Simple Embroidered Bag

Nothing is more special than a gift you've made yourself. Embellish ribbons or stitch rows and rows of decorative stitches across the front of the fabric for this very simple bag. Don't limit your creativity by making the pattern just like it looks on the envelope—make it your own!

Gather your supplies:

- A simple bag pattern (such as Butterick #3056)- see pattern envelope back for fabric suggestions and quantities
- 1/2 yard of lining fabric—cotton or cotton/polyester to coordinate
- 1/2 yard of heavyweight fusible interfacing
- 3/8 yard of 1 3/4"-wide ribbon for pocket trim
- #30-40 wt. rayon or metallic thread in assorted colors
- Polyester sewing thread
- Pins
- Sewing scissors
- Ruler
- Fabric marking pencil, pen, or chalk
- Dual-feed foot (optional accessory)

Let's get started:

1

Begin this project by reading the information about patterns beginning on page 126. Following the pattern guide sheet, cut the bag from the fabric and interfacing. Note: We have omitted the zipper closure on the inside pocket

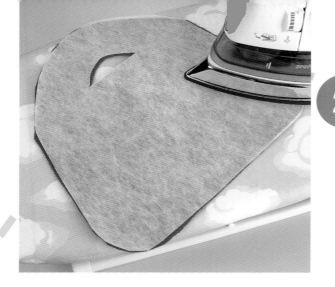

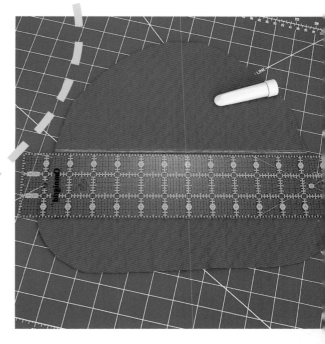

2 Following the manufacturer's instructions, fuse the interfacing to the front and back sections of the bag.

Using a ruler and fabric chalk, draw a straight line horizontally across the front bag section.

3

4

Attach a dual-feed foot, if available, and quilting guide to the sewing machine. Using a rayon thread, begin stitching on the marked line with a decorative stitch. Continue stitching parallel lines of pretty stitches across the front of the bag varying the thread colors as desired. The quilting guide will help keep the rows even.

Continued

Just Sew You Know

When working with a pre-quilted fabric, you can use the quilting lines as your stitching guides.

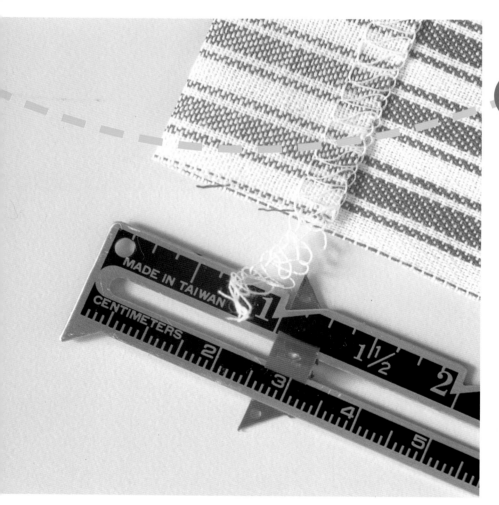

5

Construct the outside of the bag according to the guide sheet.

For an inside pocket, cut a pocket section 7" × 8" from the lining fabric. Serge-finish the upper edge of the pocket. Fold the upper edge down 1" to the right side.

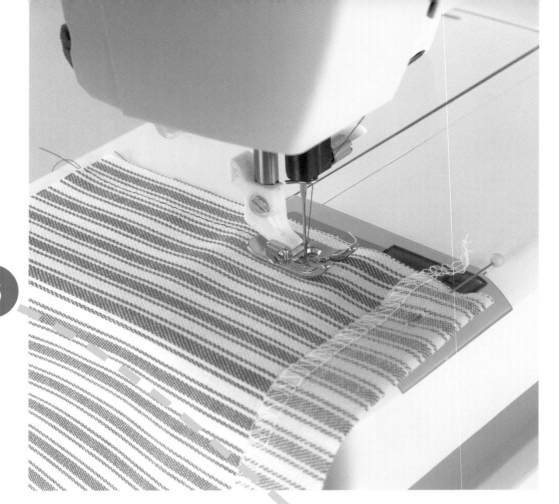

6 Stitch ¹/2" from the cut edge along each side.

7 Trim across the corners. Turn the upper edge to the inside and press. Press under along the stitching lines on each side.

Continued

8

Fold both the pocket and lining pieces in half and mark the center at the bottom edge. Pin the pocket to the lining piece, matching the marks.

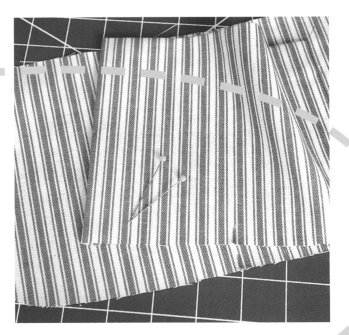

9

Sew the pocket to the lining very close to the edge on the sides. Reinforce the upper corners by backstitching.

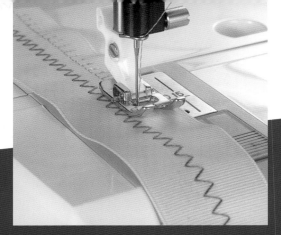

Use ribbon to create a one-of-a-kind trim for the outside of your bag. Fuse a strip of fusible web to one side of the ribbon. Attach the dual-feed foot and decorate the ribbon with a variety of stitches. Sew the ribbon to the outside of the bag using a narrow satin stitch along the lengthwise edges.

Stitch the lining to the bag and complete bag following the guide sheet.

Terry Cloth Sports Towel

What better gift for that active, sports-minded family member or friend than this handy, personalized towel made by YOU! It will hold your keys or ID while absorbing perspiration.

Gather your supplies:

- 1 purchased hand towel
- 3/4 yard of cotton fabric
- 1 1/2 yards of coordinating 5/8"-wide grosgrain ribbon
- 1/2 yard of Velcro™ Sew-On hook and loop tape
- Polyester sewing thread
- Sewing scissors
- Pins

Let's get started:

1 Measure the hand towel and cut the cotton fabric the same size.

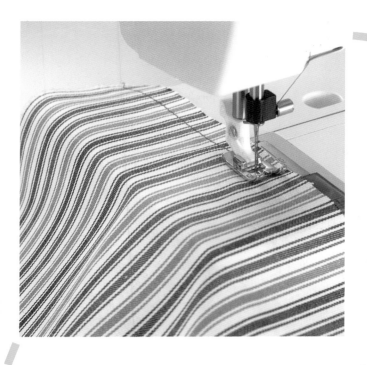

2

Stitch ½" from the cut edges of the lining, using a very long stitch length. This is called basting.

3

Press under along all the cut edges using the stitching lines as guides.

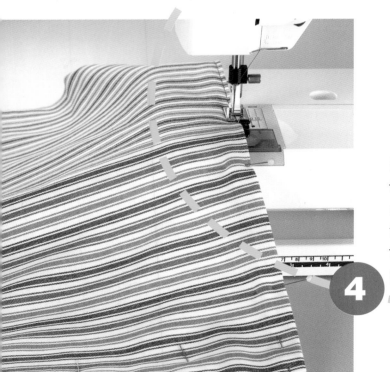

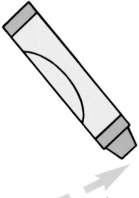

4

Layer the fabric over the towel with the wrong side down and pin. Stitch the fabric to the towel close to the edges removing the pins as you sew.

Continued

5

Fold up 6" along one end to form a pocket. Mark the top edge of the pocket on the terry cloth with pins.

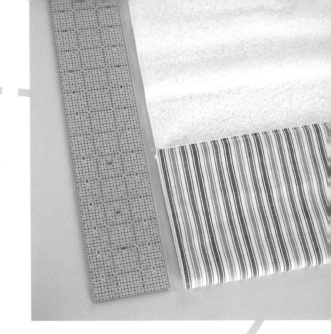

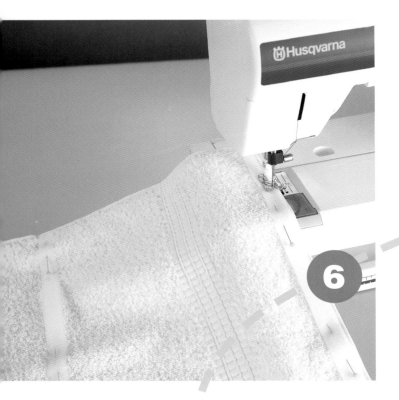

6

Pin the hook side of the Velcro® Sew-On hook and loop tape at the pin markings and pin the loop portion on the towel side at the upper edge of the pocket. Stitch along the edges of the tapes.

Cut three lengths of ribbon the width of the towel plus 1". Pin one piece to the upper edge of the pocket on the fabric side and pin the remaining pieces along the decorative band on the towel side turning under 1/2" at each end. Stitch close to the edges through all thicknesses.

7

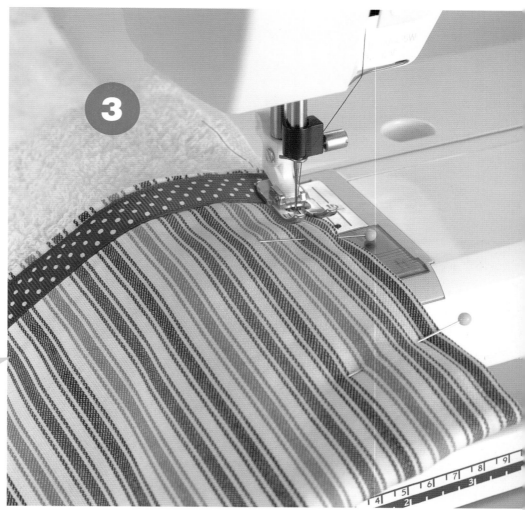

3

Fold up the pocket so the hook and loop tape meet. Stitch along the sides to close the pocket.

8

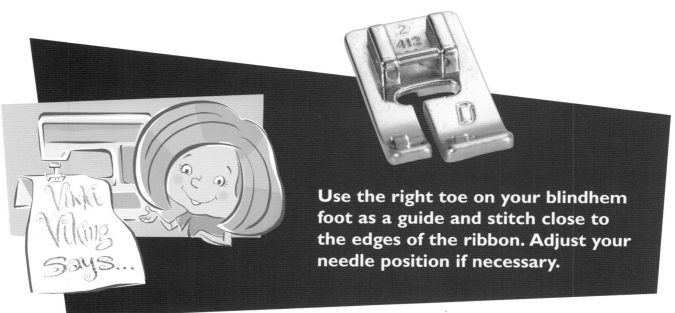

Vikki Viking Says...

Use the right toe on your blindhem foot as a guide and stitch close to the edges of the ribbon. Adjust your needle position if necessary.

Potpourri Coasters

Add the sweet smell of spice to Grandma's cup of tea or coffee with these simple-to-make coasters. Choose your favorite flavor to fill the shapes and the hot cup or mug will release the potpourri scent when placed upon it.

Gather your supplies:

- ¼ yard or remnants of pre-quilted fabrics
- ¼ yard of organdy or sheer fabric
- Potpourri of choice (small pieces preferable)
- Pattern tracing material
- Sewing scissors
- Polyester sewing thread
- Pinking shears
- Fabric marking pencil, or tracing paper and wheel

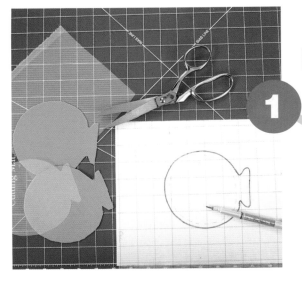

Let's get started:

1 Trace the patterns copied from the CD onto pattern tracing material. (See page 56.) Cut one each from the pre-quilted and one from the sheer fabrics. Trace the stitching line on the wrong side of the pre-quilted fabric with a fabric marking pencil.

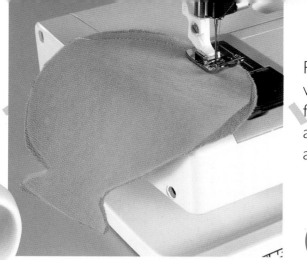

Place the sheer fabric on the wrong side of the pre-quilted fabric and pin in place. Stitch along the stitching line leaving a 2" opening for filling.

2

3

Fill the coaster with potpourri being sure not to overfill. Stitch the opening closed, remembering to backstitch at the beginning and end.

Using the pinking shears, trim around the edges to finish and also keep the fabric from raveling. Learn more about pinking shears on page 59.

4

Warm Fleecy Scarf

Make a soft fleece scarf for someone in need. Add fun ball-fringe trim and a monogram or embroidered design as a special touch.

STITCHES *that* SERVE

Gather your supplies:

- 1½ yards each of two colors of fleece
- 1½ yards of ball fringe
- Pattern tracing material
- Sewing scissors
- Fabric marking pencil, pen, or chalk
- Ruler or seam gauge
- Polyester sewing thread
- Pins
- Fusible letters for monogram
- Iron
- Hand-sewing needle

Let's get started:

1

Print the scarf pattern from the CD. (See page 56.) Trace the paper pattern onto pattern tracing material. Cut two scarf pieces from the fleece using the pattern. Using a marking pencil and seam gauge, mark 5/8" seamlines on the fleece inside the edges.

2

Fuse a letter to one end of the scarf according to the manufacturer's instructions. A pressing cloth may be necessary as heat from the iron could melt or leave a mark on the fleece.

Just Sew You Know

Be sure to position the letter so the top is toward the body of the scarf.

Continued

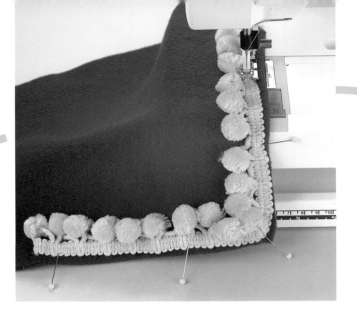

3

Pin the ball fringe to the right side of one scarf piece at each point, 1/2" from the edge. Baste in place using a long stitch length.

Just Sew You Know

Underneath the soft surface, fleece is a knitted fabric. The best choice of needle for a knit is a ballpoint, stretch or universal needle. Match the size of the needle to the weight of your fabric—the heavier the fleece, the larger size of needle. For most weights of fleece, an 80/12 or 90/14 needle is a good choice.

Pin the two scarf sections, right sides together, and stitch along the seamline, leaving an opening on one long side for turning. Trim across the corners and turn to the right side. Lightly press with a cool iron.

4

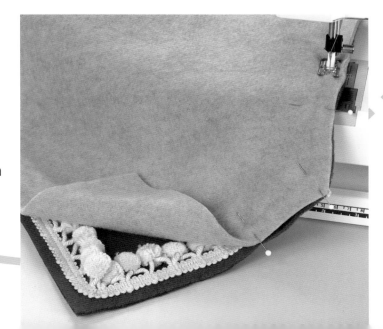

Just Sew You Know

Heat from an iron could possibly melt or leave a mark on fleece. Since seams and seam allowances cannot be pressed flat, trim away the seam allowance and topstitch along the edge to define the seams of your fleece projects.

5

Take small stitches through both edges of the fabric, slipstitching the opening closed with a hand needle and thread.

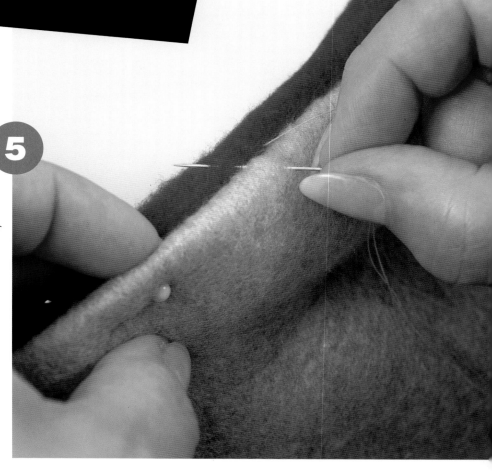

Who's Got a Notion?

Handmade Ornaments
(page 68)

Soft, Flannel Receiving Blanket
(page 82)

Sewing Exercises— Using Notions

Follow the instructions here for practice exercises in using new notions.

Begin by copying the pattern "It's a Star!" from the CD to your printer. After taping the pieces together, use your pattern tracing material and trace the star onto the grided material. Set your seam gauge to $1/2$" and draw a stitching line on the new pattern inside the cutting line. You have now learned how to transfer a pattern and add a seam allowance.

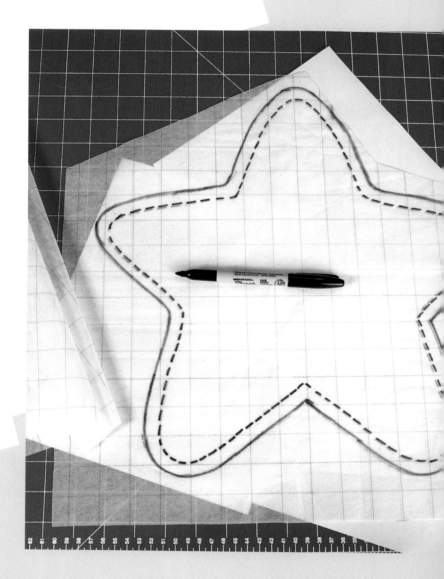

You will now learn how to sew on a button by machine. Take two layers of cotton fabric and a 2-holed button. Remove the presser foot sole (check your instruction manual for exact directions for your machine) and set your stitch length to 0. Remember to lower the presser foot lever—this engages the thread tension. Set your zig zag stitch to a width of 3. Carefully lower the needle into one hole of the button. Turn the handwheel slowly and check to be sure the zig zag width is correct and the needle goes into the other hole without hitting the button. Adjust the stitch width if necessary.

Continued

Important Notions

There are many types of tools or "notions." As you try different ones, you will begin to choose your favorites. But don't be afraid to try different marking tools, cutting tools, or rulers. We are describing specific notions here. Practice using them on scraps of fabric before you begin your first project. Watch the video section on the CD for more information.

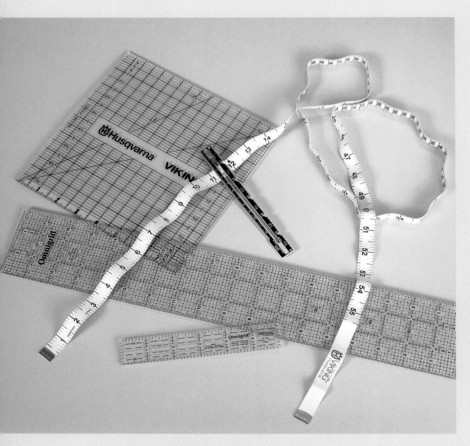

Accurate measurements are the key to successful sewing projects. A variety of measuring tools are used when sewing.

A cloth tape measure is used for taking body measurements or measuring curved areas.

A yardstick measures one yard—36"—and is used for measuring fabric and straight lines.

Use a seam gauge when measuring hem allowances at the edge of a garment or in shorter areas. There is a movable arrow on the gauge that you set to the measurement you choose.

Clear plastic rulers and grids are used for accurately measuring and marking fabric. Designed originally for quilting, these rulers are perfect for all types of sewing. Clear rulers also come in a variety of lengths and widths.

Marking tools are used for transferring important marks to your fabric, such as darts, tucks, stitching lines, or center front lines. These pens, pencils, and chalk markers are designed for use on fabric since the marks created are not permanent and may be easily removed. Many of the markers are water-soluble, air-soluble, or can be brushed away with little effort.

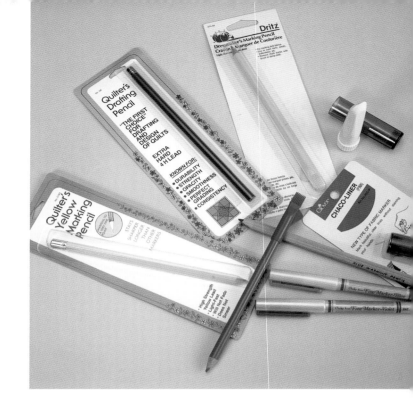

We are using pinking shears for a number of the projects in this section. They are similar to scissors, but create a "zig zag" cutting edge instead of a straight one. Use pinking sheers to trim the edge of your fabric and prevent fraying. Pinking shears may also be used on many projects for creating an exposed, decorative edge. As you cut, realign the scissor's teeth around the pattern pieces so the zig zag effect is even.

It's a Heart, Moon, Star, Pine Tree, or Snowman Pillow

Share a memory with a friend and make a felt autograph pillow for yourself in one of many shapes. If you want the pillow bigger, just enlarge the pattern on a photocopier.

Gather your supplies:

- ¹/₂ yard of felt for each pillow (small pieces for snowman's hat and nose)
- Assorted flat buttons
- Polyester fiberfill
- Pattern tracing material
- Dressmaker's tracing paper and tracing wheel
- Scotch-brand Magic Tape™
- Pinking shears
- Sewing scissors
- Polyester sewing thread
- Pins

Let's get started:

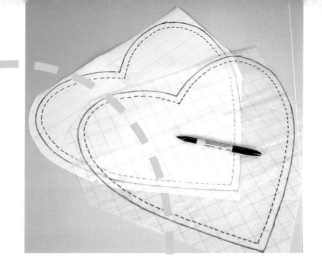

1

Copy the pattern from the CD and trace it onto pattern tracing material. Pin the pattern to the felt and cut around the outer edge of the heart pattern with your pinking shears. Cut two pieces of felt.

Just Sew You Know

Once you've made the first cut into the felt, reposition the pinking shears so the jagged edge of the blade matches the previously cut edge. This will help to keep the zig zag edge continuous.

Transfer the seamline from the pattern onto the heart pieces using the tracing paper and tracing wheel.

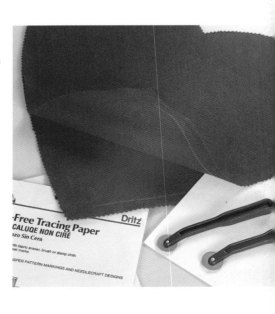

2

Continued

Tape buttons 1 1/2" from the pinked edge around one heart piece. Set your sewing machine to a zig zag stitch, lower the feed dogs and remove the presser foot. Carefully position the button under the needle and adjust the stitch width (approximately 3mm) so the needle goes in and out of the button holes. Stitch in and out of the holes several times. Carefully remove the tape.

③

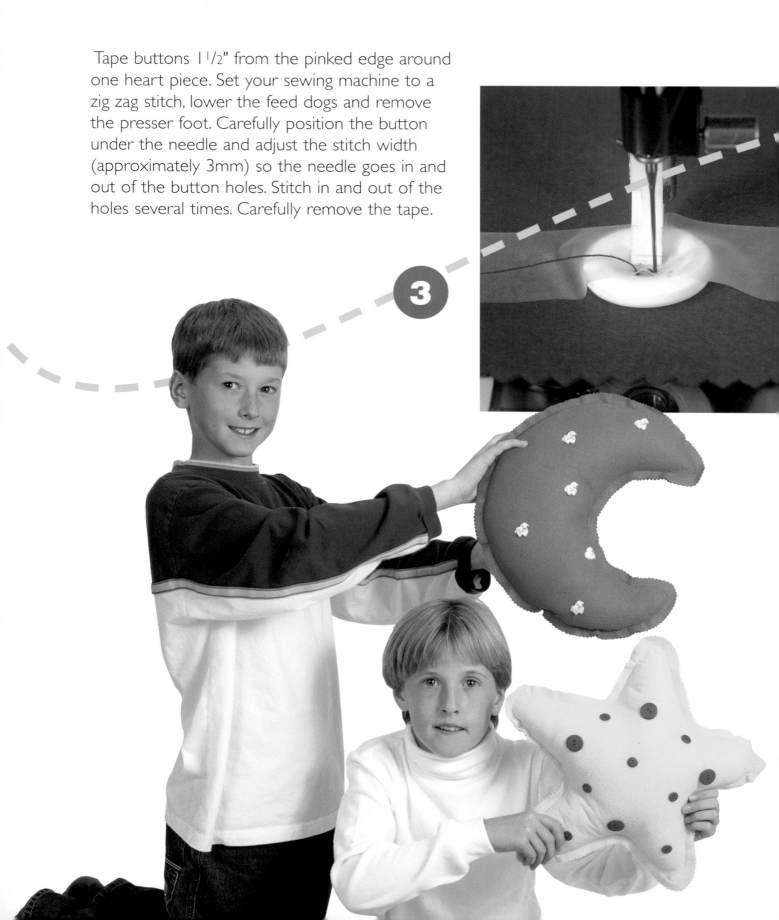

4

Pin the two heart pieces, wrong sides together, and stitch along the marking. Leave a 3"-4" opening to stuff.

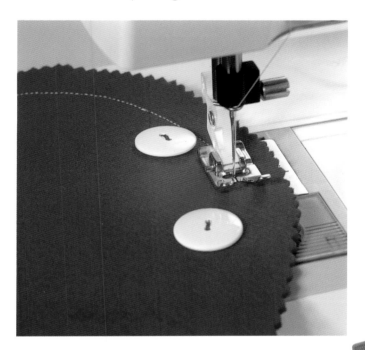

5

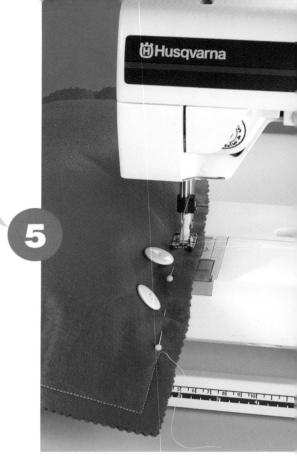

Stuff the pillow with the fiberfill. Pin the open edges together and stitch closed. You just made a heart pillow! Now try the other shapes.

Vikki Viking Says...

When sewing on a button, use a clearance plate under the button to give more space between the button and the fabric. The longer thread that is produced makes it easier to button heavy fabrics.

It's My Diary

Cover a blank book or memory album with fabric and a special, photo-transferred picture personalizing it just for you! This easy project also makes a great gift for a friend. Add stamp designs, buttons, and trim.

Gather your supplies:

- Photo album or diary
- Felt
- Pinking shears
- Photo transfer paper or stamp and paint (or ink pad)
- Ribbon
- Assorted buttons
- Contrasting decorative thread
- Tape measure
- Fabric marking pencil, pen, or chalk
- Ruler
- Pins

Let's get started:

1 Using a tape measure, measure around the photo album or diary. Add 1" to the width and length measurement. Measure and mark the fabric using these measurements; cut out using the pinking shears. For the flap sections, mark the fabric the height of the book plus 1" x 2½" wide. Cut out two flaps using the pinking shears.

Cut two 10" pieces of ribbon for the ties. Find the center of each side of the cover and pin a ribbon piece on each inside edge. Pin the flap sections to each end sandwiching the ribbon between the flap and the cover.

2

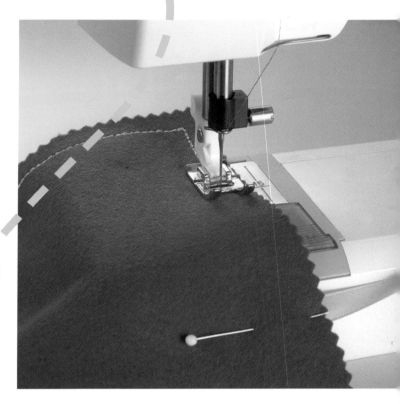

Using a decorative thread and a long stitch length, stitch around the entire cover $1/2$" from the cut edges.

3

Just Sew You Know

If your machine has a reinforced straight stitch, a stitch that sews back and forth in a stright line, use that stitch around the edge of your book cover. It creates a heavy topstitching effect. Remember to use a longer stitch length for the best decorative look.

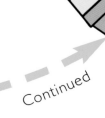

Continued

Choose a special photograph and print it on colorfast fabric sheets following the manufacturer's instructions. Trim the photo to fit, if necessary.

4

Apply the picture to the front of your album cover using a zig zag stitch. Add ribbon decoration over the edges. Or add a design by applying ink to a stamp and placing it on the book cover.

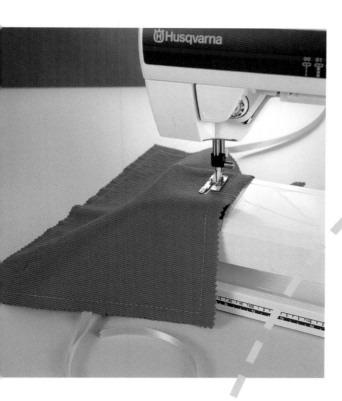

6

Embellish the cover with special buttons and trims, as desired. Thread the ribbon through the buttonholes and tie the ends on the front.

5

Place the book cover on the book. On the front, measure in ¹/₂" from the front spine edge and 1" from the top and bottom edges, marking at the top and bottom. Remove the cover and stitch two buttonholes beginning at these marks.

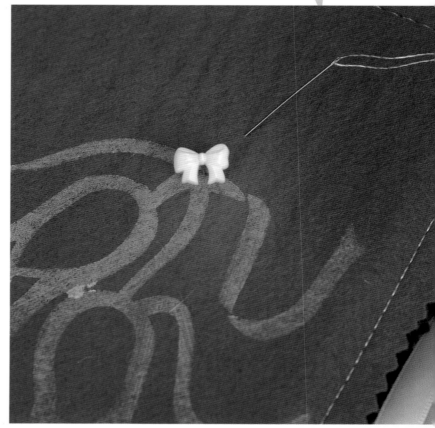

Handmade Ornaments

Give a little bit of yourself with these "handmade" ornaments perfect for any season.

Gather your supplies:

- Two 9" X 12" rectangles of felt
- Sewing scissors
- Dressmaker's tracing paper and tracing wheel
- Pinking shears
- Polyester sewing thread
- Seam gauge
- Floral wire
- Pattern tracing material
- Buttons, flowers, ribbon, etc. for decorating
- Hand-sewing needle

Let's get started:

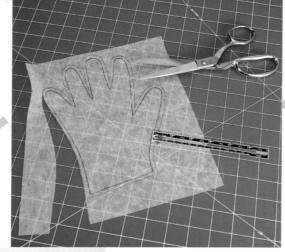

1

Trace your hand on pattern tracing material. Add a ¹/4" seam allowance to the outside edge.

2

Trace the outline of the pattern onto one piece of felt. Pin two layers of felt together placing the pins in the fingers to hold the layers together. Cut on the lines with your pinking shears.

3

Cut a 15"-long piece of wire for the hanger. Fold the wire in half and twist the wires together 1" from the center. Curl the center over your finger to create a hanger. Separate the ends.

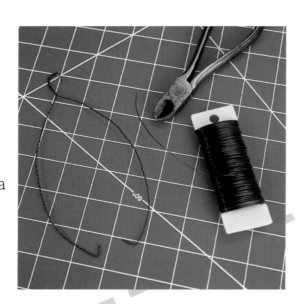

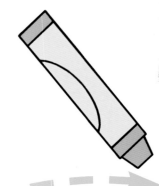

Continued

Try other wire hanger options. Curl the wire with a pencil; use the sharpened end for really small curls. Kink the wire with small, random folds, or wrap and shape wire-edged ribbon around the hanger.

4

Decide how you want to decorate the ornament. If what you will be adding can be sewn on by machine and will not be in the way as you sew around the fingers, add the decorations first. If you are adding buttons, flowers, or other dimensional items, sew them to the ornament with a hand-sewing needle and thread.

Insert one end of the wire between the layers of felt, through the seam $1/2$" from the open end of the ornament. Push 1" of the wire through the seam. Fold the cut end of the wire toward the hanger. Twist the wires together above the pinked edge of the ornament. Repeat for the other side of the ornament.

5

Use a $1/4$" seam allowance to sew around the pinked edge of the ornament, leaving the top edge open. Guide the edge of the presser foot along the edge for the perfect seam allowance. Remember to backstitch at the beginning and end of your seam.

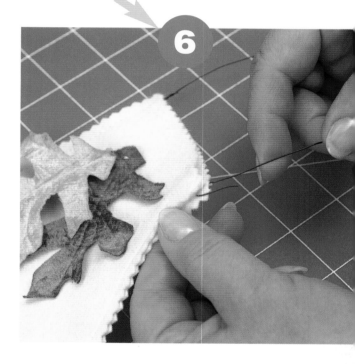

6

Just Sew You Know

Decorate the ordinary for an extraordinary result, adding special trims to a project for a truly unique look. Embellishment can be as simple as adding a few buttons and as involved as sewing sequins or beads. Appliqué and embroidery are two decorative examples.

A Christmas Stocking for Your Pet

Treat your pet on a special holiday with his own Christmas stocking. Filled with doggie treats he will be your faithful friend forever!

Gather your supplies:

- ½ yard of green felt; 9"X12" pieces each of tan and red felt for band and bone
- Paw print stamp
- Stamp pad
- Pattern tracing material
- Sewing scissors
- Pinking shears
- Polyester sewing thread
- Fabric marking pencil, pen, or chalk
- Pins

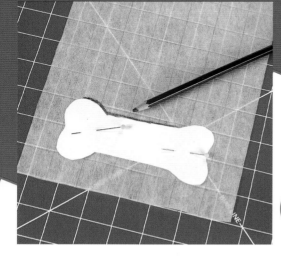

1

Let's get started:

Print the stocking and bone patterns off the CD and trace onto pattern tracing material.

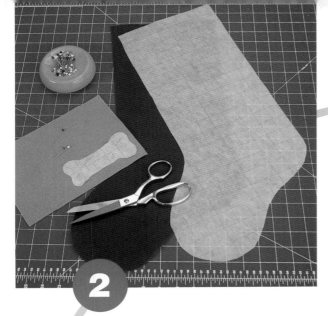

Use your pinking shears to pink around the outside of the stocking sections and band leaving the upper edge a straight edge. Pink around the edges of the bone and the hanger.

2

Cut the stocking from green felt. Cut two bands, 3" × 8", and one hanger, 3/4" × 8", from red felt and cut the bone from the tan felt.

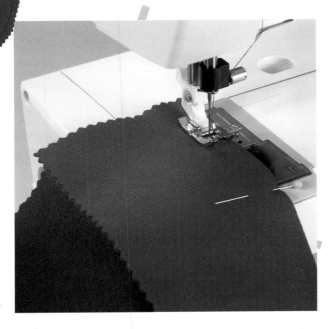

Pin the band to the upper edge of both stocking sections. Stitch 1/4" from the edge across the top edges through both layers. Fold the hanger strip in half lengthwise. Pin and stitch the hanger to the inside upper edge of one stocking piece.

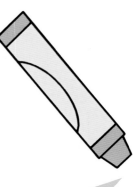

4

Continued

5

Pin the bone to the front stocking section as pictured. Stitch 1/4" from the edge.

6

Decorate the stocking using the paw print stamp and stamp pad.

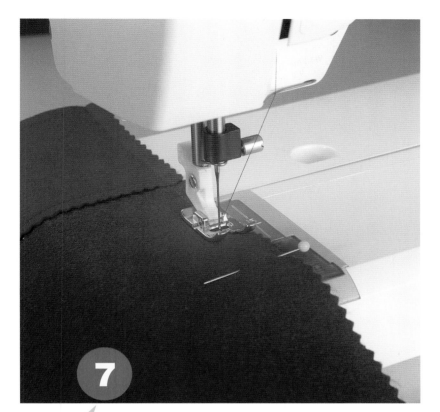

With wrong sides together, pin the front and back stocking sections together. Stitch ¹/4" from the pinked edges leaving the top open.

Pixie Viking Says...

Decorate your pet's stocking by appliquéing its name across the front. Cut the letters out with your pinking shears and stitch ¹/4" from the edge.

Handicap Tote

Sew up this handy felt tote for those disabled and using a walker. The straps attach to the bar with Velcro® tabs and can easily be adjusted. This is a great project for "Stitches that Serve."

Gather your supplies:

- ¹/₃ yard of green felt
- ¹/₃ yard of orange felt
- ¹/₄ yard of yellow felt
- 2¹/₄ yards of cotton webbing or strapping
- ⁷/₈ yard of Velcro® Sew-On hook and loop tape
- ¹/₃ yard of coordinating ribbon
- Polyester sewing thread
- Rotary cutter and mat
- Ruler
- Tape measure
- Seam gauge
- Pinking shears
- Pins
- Fabric marking pencil, pen, or chalk

Let's get started:

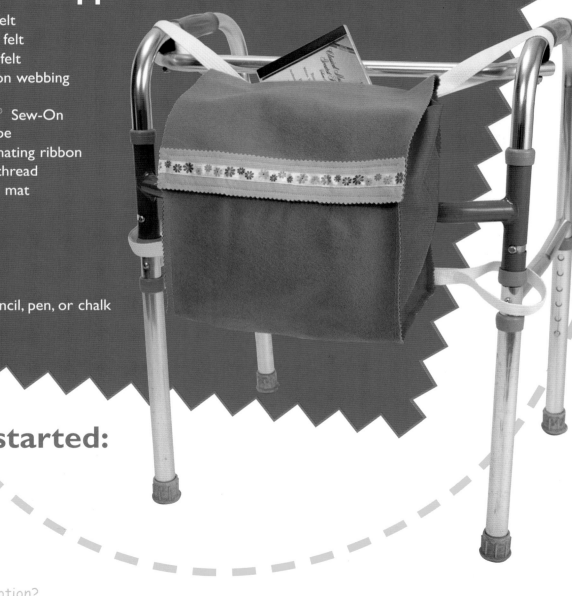

Copy the patterns from the CD for the tote. Using your rotary cutter and mat, cut from the green felt one 12" × 36" rectangle; from the orange felt, cut two 7" × 11" side rectangles; and from the yellow felt, cut one 2" × 12" rectangle and one 6" pocket square. Transfer any marks to the felt pieces with your marking pen. On the yellow felt pieces, pink one long side of the rectangle and pink three sides of the square.

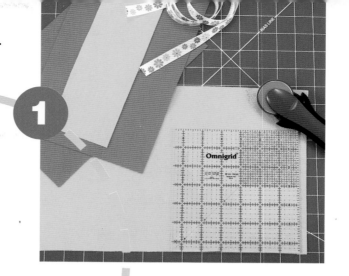

1

2 From the cotton webbing, cut four 20"-long pieces. From the Velcro® Sew-On hook and loop tape, cut four 7" pieces and three 1" pieces.

3

On one end of each of the four straps, fold in ¹/4", then fold the end over again so the cut edge is enclosed. Sew close to the inside folded edge.

Separate the hook from the loop part of the tape. On the wrong side, pin and sew the hook tape ¹/2" away from the hemmed edge of each strap. Measure 3" down from the end of the hook tape. Pin and sew the loop tape to each strap.

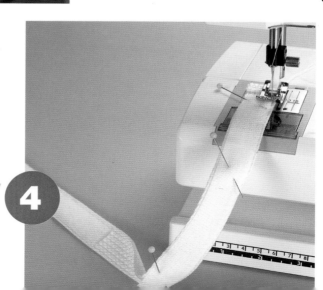

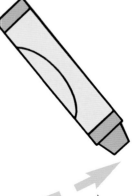

4

Continued

5

Mark the center of one short side of the green rectangle. Center one piece of the 1" hook tape over the mark and 3/4" from the edge. Pin the other pieces 2" on each side and 3/4" from the edge. Sew around the outside edge of the tape to secure.

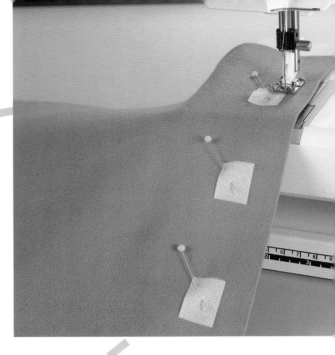

6

On the other end of the rectangle, mark the center of the opposite short side. Center one piece of 1" loop tape over the mark and 3" from the edge. Pin the other pieces 2" on each side and 3" from the edge. Sew around the outside edge of the tape.

7

Make a back pocket on the side with the hook tape nearest the edge. Find the center of the short side and measure and mark down 12". Center the yellow square over the mark with the straight edge parallel to the short side. Sew along the three pinked edges to make a pocket.

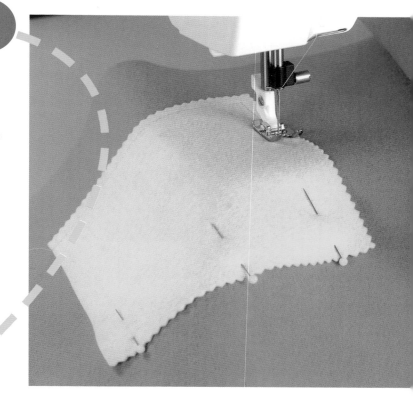

8

Pin the ribbon over the center of the narrow yellow rectangle and sew along each edge.

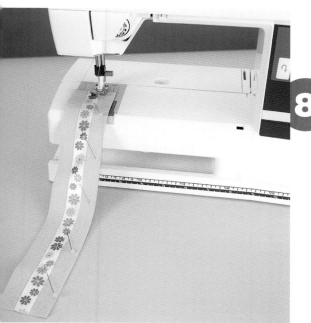

On the short end of the green rectangle with the hook side of the tape face down, pin the yellow rectangle matching the long straight edges. Sew around all four edges. Pink the long straight edge through both yellow and green layers.

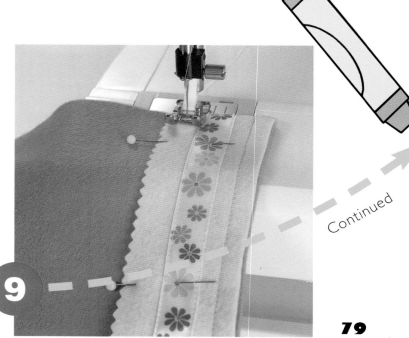

9

Continued

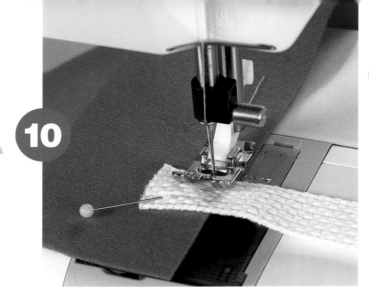

On one orange rectangle, pin a strap 1" from the corner on a long side with the Velcro® side of the strap facing the felt. Sew the strap using a 1/2" seam allowance. Repeat this step on the other orange rectangle but in the opposite corner making a right and left side for the tote.

On the long sides of the green rectangle, find the 10 1/2", 16 1/2" and 27" marks on the plain short end.

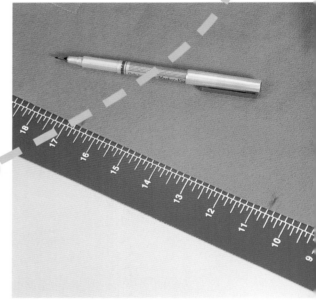

Pin an orange rectangle to the green rectangle, placing the strap between the layers of felt and matching the corners of the orange side to the marks at 10 1/2" and 16 1/2". The 27" mark indicates the top and flap of the tote. Sew the tote sides with the orange felt facing up using a 1/2" seam allowance.

14 Trim away half of the side seam allowances with the pinking shears being very careful not to cut off the straps. Continue pinking the entire length of the green rectangle.

13 When you reach the corners, stop with your needle down, lift the presser foot, and pivot the top orange felt so the felt edge is lined up with 1/2" seam allowance guide on your needle plate. Flatten the green felt underneath to prevent a tuck in the corner. Continue stitching. Repeat on the other side.

15 Sew the top straps to the back of the tote. With the Velcro® side away from tote, pin the straps 11" down from the yellow trimmed flap edge and 1" away from the pinked sides. Fold under 1/2" on the cut edge of the strap. Use a fabric marker to draw a 1" box on the straps. Sew over the lines.

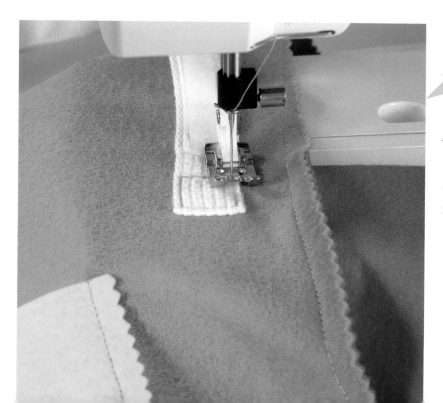

Soft, Flannel Receiving Blankets

These simple flannel blankets are a great project for a beginner sewer as well as a generous charitable contribution.

Gather your supplies:

- 1 yard each of two coordinating cotton flannel prints
- 5 yards of 1/2"-wide double-faced satin ribbon
- Polyester sewing thread
- Pinking shears
- Fabric marking pen or pencil
- Pins
- Yardstick
- Seam gauge
- Hand-sewing needle
- Glue stick (optional)

Let's get started:

1

Place the two print fabrics, wrong sides together, on a flat working surface and pin to hold the layers together. Using your fabric marking pen and a yardstick, measure and mark a 36" square.

2

Cut along the marked lines through both layers of fabric with the pinking shears.

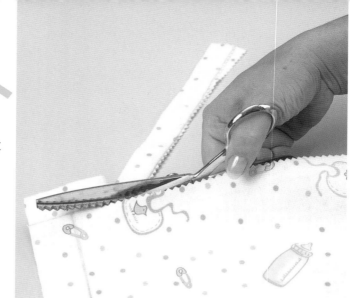

3

With your fabric marking pen and seam gauge, measure 5/8" from the cut edges and mark a seamline.

4

Set your machine for a long straight stitch (6.0 mm) and baste the layers together along the marked line.

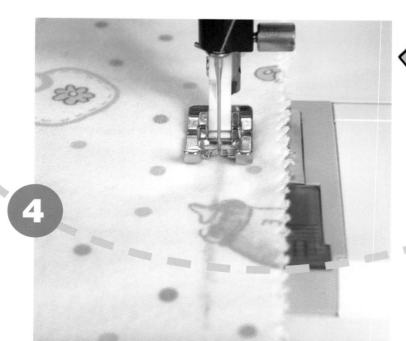

Continued

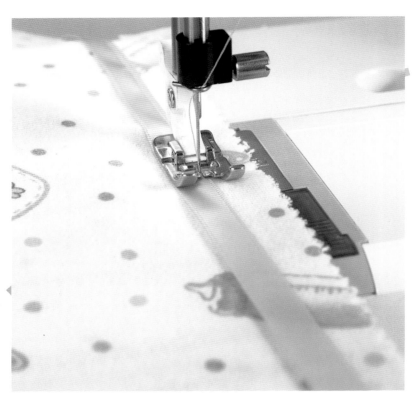

5

Place the ribbon over the basting and pin in place.

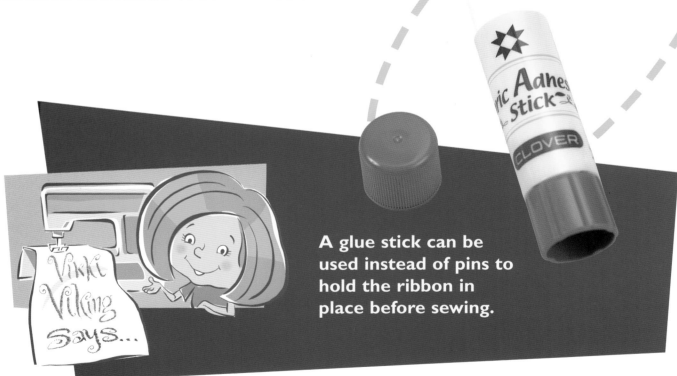

Vikki Viking Says...

A glue stick can be used instead of pins to hold the ribbon in place before sewing.

Topstitch along both edges of the ribbon using the edge of your presser foot as a guide. At the corner, miter the ribbon by folding the ribbon back onto itself and pressing. Then fold the ribbon diagonally so it covers the basting line on the next side. Press the corner again and continue stitching.

6

7

Cut four 12" strips of ribbon and tie each strip into a bow. Hand-stitch a bow at each corner of the blanket with a needle and thread.

Teach Me How to Quilt!

Teach Me

Sewing Exercises— Understanding Piecing and Quilting

Learning how to quilt can be lots of fun! You need to understand some important terms before you begin. You will get a chance to practice these techniques when you start sewing the projects in this section.

Usually a quilt is made from a lot of smaller pieces of fabric sewn together. That technique is call **piecing or patchwork.** Here is where you can be really creative and have fun mixing fabric designs and colors. You also get to decide what kind of design you want to make. The more piecing you do, the more complicated your designs can become.

Once you have sewn all the pieces together for the top, you will add the batting, the soft stuffing in the middle **(B)**. Sandwich the batting between the pieced top **(A)** and the backing **(C)** and pin the layers together with quilting pins. Sew the layers together.

After the layers are sewn together, you can begin quilting! **Quilting** is the process of adding stitches to keep all the layers from shifting. Your quilting stitches can be done in straight lines or in beautiful, intricate designs. Make a quilted pillow or throw for yourself and have fun doing it too!

How to Quilt!

B ———— A

C

Continued

Important Quilting Tools

There are specific tools and notions used for piecing and quilting. The CD video explains many of these notions for you.

To sew a perfect 1/4" seam on a quilt, attach a 1/4" or piecing-patchwork foot to your machine. This foot is designed so the needle is exactly 1/4" away from the edge of the foot. Set your sewing machine to a straight stitch and place the fabric under the foot so the edge is even with the right side of the presser foot toe and begin sewing. Guide the fabric next to the right toe for your 1/4" seams. If you don't have a 1/4" foot available, move the needle 1/4" away from the edge of the foot or mark the needle plate.

Many quilt designs use squares, triangles, or other shaped pieces. Make more permanent templates from plastic template sheets or cardboard to be used over and over again. Then trace around the template with a marking pencil directly onto your fabric.

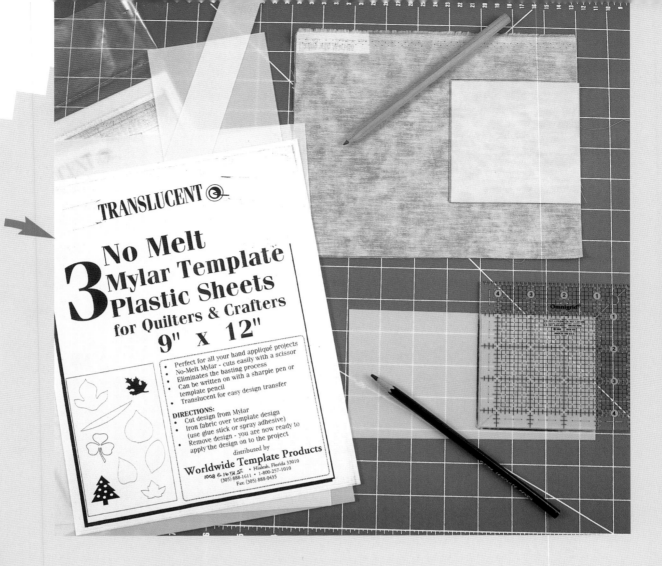

TRANSLUCENT

3 No Melt Mylar Template Plastic Sheets

for Quilters & Crafters

9" x 12"

- Perfect for all your hand appliqué projects
- No-Melt Mylar - cuts easily with a scissor
- Eliminates the basting process
- Can be written on with a sharpie pen or template pencil
- Translucent for easy design transfer

DIRECTIONS:
- Cut design from Mylar
- Iron fabric over template design (use glue stick or spray adhesive)
- Remove design - you are now ready to apply the design on to the project

distributed by

Worldwide Template Products
1008 E. 16TH ST. • Hialeah, Florida 33010
(305) 888-1611 • 1-800-257-1010
Fax (305) 888-0435

Another very useful presser foot to own is a dual-feed foot. The rubber feet on the underside of this presser foot work with the feed dogs on the sewing machine so all of the layers will feed evenly while stitching. Use a dual-feed foot for stitching the layers of your quilt project and also for matching plaids and stripes.

Other important quilting tools are a rotary cutter, mat, and ruler. Watch the video for information on how to use these tools safely.

An Easy, Quilted Bed Throw

Spruce up your room with this pieced bed throw. Use six different fabrics for the front squares and three coordinating fabrics for the back. Combine with the Crazy Patch Pillows and you'll have a newly decorated room that you made yourself!

Gather your supplies:

- $1/2$ yard each of six fabrics for front blocks
- $2^1/2$ yards each of three fabrics for back sections
- Cotton batting (single bed size)
- 10 large decorative buttons
- Polyester sewing thread
- Sewing scissors
- Pins
- Edge joining foot
- Clear plastic ruler

Let's get started:

1

From the three 2½-yard pieces, cut one strip each 24½" X 88½" for the back section. From each of the ½-yard pieces, cut two 16½" X 16½" square blocks.

2

Arrange the blocks in 4 rows with 3 columns, mixing the colors or prints to make your design for the pieced top.

3

For all seams for patchwork, you use a ¼" seam allowance. Take two square blocks, right sides together, and sew one side. Complete the row by adding the third block. Repeat this procedure until all four rows are sewn. Press all the seam allowances in one direction.

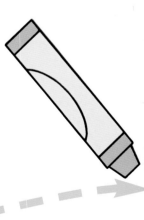

Sew the rows together starting at the top row, matching the seams. Alternating the direction of the seam allowances will help in matching the corners of the blocks.

4

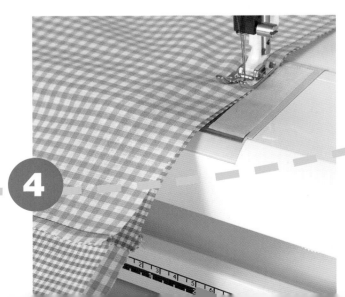

Continued

Batting comes in many lofts or thicknesses. Choose the loft you want for your bed throw depending on how fluffy you want the quilt to be.

5 Place two quilt-back strips, wrong sides together, matching the long sides and sew. Add the third strip to complete the back. Press the seam allowances in one direction.

6 Lay the quilt back on a large flat surface, right side down. Place the batting over the back allowing 6½" of the backing to extend beyond on all sides. Trim the batting as necessary. Lay the quilt top, right side up, 6" inside the batting on all sides. Pin through all layers of the quilt.

Using an edge-joining foot, stitch right in the seam of the blocks all across the top. Backstitch at the beginning and end of your seams. Baste the layers together 1/4" in from the quilt-top edge.

7

Continued

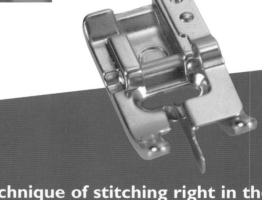

Vikki Viking Says...

The technique of stitching right in the seam is called "stitch-in-the-ditch." This technique is often used for quilting as well as in garment construction to hide the stitching. Use the guide on the edge-joining foot to separate the seam and help you stitch straight.

8

Press under ¹/4"
on all four edges
of the quilt back.

9

Wrap the pressed edge of the quilt back
over the batting up to the basting stitch
on the quilt top to form a binding and pin.
At each corner, fold the binding diagonally
so it is even with the batting edge; press.
Continue wrapping the quilt back over to
the basting stitch. You have made a mock
mitered corner.

Select a zig zag stitch (W–4-5 and L–2.5-3) to sew the edge of the binding down. At the mock mitered corners, use a straight stitch to sew along the folded diagonal edge. Remove any basting stitches that show.

10

11

Sew decorative buttons in the corners of the binding and the blocks to hold the layers together.

Crazy Patch Pillows

What a fun way to learn patchwork! Randomly add strips of fabric around a center piece to make your design. Make it your very own by mixing and matching your fabrics. This is a great scrap bag project!

Gather your supplies:

- $1/3$ yard each of five different cotton fabrics for top piecing
- $3/4$ yards of cotton for backing and top piecing
- $2/3$ yard of muslin
- 18" pillow form
- Velcro® Sew-On hook and loop tape
- Polyester sewing thread
- Sewing scissors
- Rotary cutter and mat
- Clear plastic ruler
- Fabric marking pencil or chalk
- Template material or cardboard
- Manila folder

Let's get started:

1

Cut one 10" X 19" rectangle and one 14" x 19" rectangle from the $3/4$ yard of cotton. Use the leftover fabric for crazy patch strips. From the muslin, cut one 21" square for the piecing foundation. From the Velcro® Sew-On hook and loop tape, cut three 1" pieces.

Copy the center piece from the CD and make a template from cardboard or template material. Trace the template on one fabric with a fabric marking pencil or chalk. Cut out one piece.

2

3

Select six different fabrics. Stacking three or four fabrics at a time, trim away the selvedge with your rotary cutter. Cut uneven strips of the fabric that vary from 1¹/2"-2¹/2" wide on one end to 3-4" on the opposite end. Use the grid lines on the cutting mat to help you angle your ruler. Once you've made your first cut, change the angle of the ruler.

4

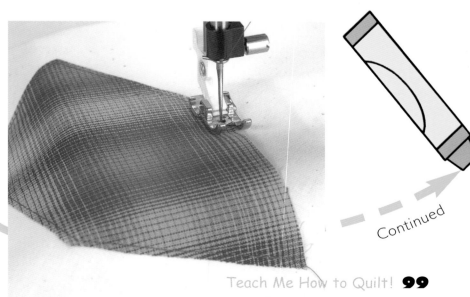

Pin the center piece, right side up, in the center of the piecing foundation muslin. Sew around the five-sided piece close to the cut edge.

Continued

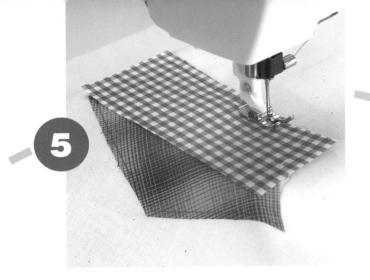

5

Along one edge of the center patch, lay a strip, right side down, lining up the cut edges and extending the strip at least 1" beyond. Stitch the strip down with a ¼" seam allowance, stopping at the corner of the center patch. Open out the strip and press away from the center patch. Line up the ruler with the edge of the center patch and sewn strip. Draw a line extending the edge. Trim the excess fabric.

Just Sew You Know

To get the best result, take time to press each strip after you stitched it down to the center patch.

6

Turn the center patch one turn and add a second different strip, right side down, over the center patch. Generously overlap the edges of the center patch including the first strip you added. Sew the second strip to the center patch and first strip. Press the strip away from the center patch.

After each strip is added, line up the ruler with the edge of the center patch and extend the line with a fabric marking pencil. Trim away the excess fabric.

7

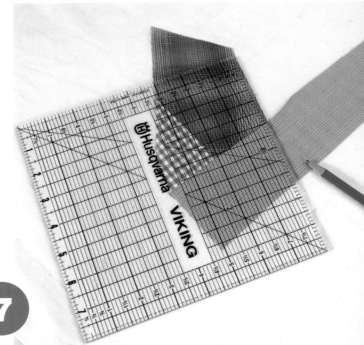

8

Continue adding strips around the center patch always turning the muslin foundation in the same direction one turn. As you add strips to the center patch, alternate the size of the strip to keep the piecing looking random.

9 Add strips around the center patch until the foundation muslin is completely covered. Trim the pieced top to a 19" block.

Continued

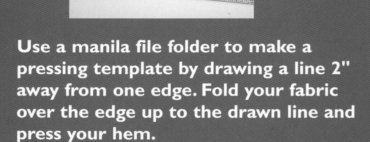

Use a manila file folder to make a pressing template by drawing a line 2" away from one edge. Fold your fabric over the edge up to the drawn line and press your hem.

Vinki Viking Says...

10

On one 19" side of each back piece, press under 2" to the wrong side. Open out the pressed edge and fold the cut edge into the crease, making a 1" double-fold hem.

11

Pin and topstitch close to the folded edge. Move your needle position if necessary.

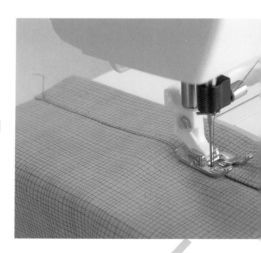

12 Find the center of the smaller back piece by folding the short sides together. Mark with a pin along the hemmed edge.

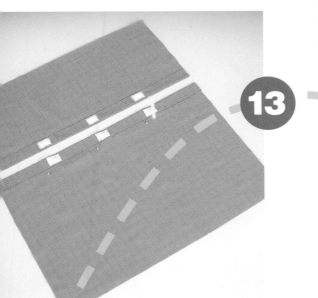

13 Separate the 1" pieces of hook and loop tape from each other. Pin one loop piece over the center pin on the wrong side of the small back piece. Pin the remaining two loop pieces 3$\frac{1}{2}$" away from the center piece. On your work surface, place the larger back piece, wrong side down, opposite the small back piece and pin the hook pieces in the hem allowance to match the loop pieces. Stitch the pieces in place on both back pieces.

Overlap the back fabric pieces so the hook and loop sticks together. With right sides together, pin the pillow front to the pillow back. Sew all four sides with a $\frac{1}{2}$" seam allowance.

14

15

Trim the corners and turn the pillow cover to the right side. Press and insert your pillow form.

Travel Checkerboard

Travel with your own checkerboard and checkers in its travel bag. What a fun gift to give a friend to take on their next summer vacation!

Gather your supplies:

- ¹/₂ yard each of four or five coordinating print fabrics for the squares, checkers, backing, and bag
- ¹/₂ yard of cotton batting
- Polyester sewing thread
- Pins
- Small beans, lentils, or split peas for filling checkers
- Piece of heavy cardboard
- Piece of paper
- Sewing scissors
- Pinking shears
- Fabric marking pencil, pen, or chalk
- Ruler
- Safety pins
- Bodkin (optional)

1 Let's get started:

Copy the 3¹/₂"-square pattern from the CD. Trace and cut one square from the cardboard.

2

Using a fabric-marking pen, trace the square onto each of two coordinating print fabrics for the checkerboard. Cut 32 squares from each fabric along the markings.

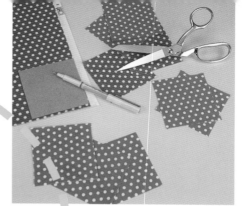

Just Sew You Know

It is important to use a straight grainline when piecing fabrics. Before you begin, straighten the fabric selvedge edges by lining them up on a cutting mat. If the ends are crooked, cut to straighten them.

3

With two squares of contrasting fabric, right sides together, mark a 1/4" seam allowance on one cut edge.

Continued

Vikki Viking Says...

To keep the seam allowances all the same size for piecing, purchase a 1/4" foot and guide the fabric along the edge. Each seam will be an accurate 1/4" wide.

4

Using a straight stitch, stitch the two squares together using the marked line as your guide. Keep stitching squares together alternating the fabrics to form strips of eight squares. You will need a total of eight strips for the complete checkerboard.

Press the seam allowances on all the strips to one side in the same direction. Alternate the direction of the seams for each row.

5

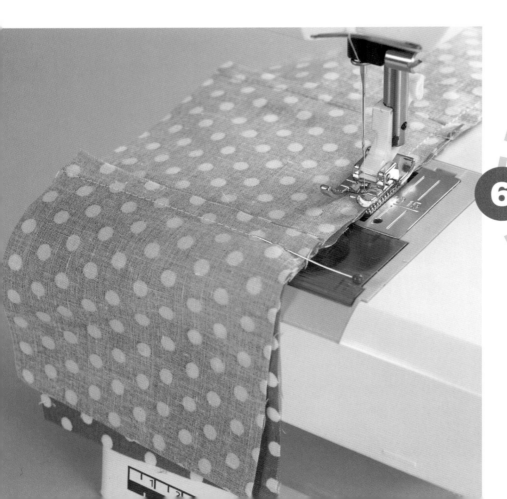

6

With right sides together, match the seams on two rows making sure the edges are even. Stitch and press the seams to one side.

Place a 24" x 24" piece of cotton batting on your work surface and layer the checkerboard backing on top, right side up. Next, layer the pieced checkerboard top, wrong side up, matching all the cut edges. Pin all the layers together. Trim away any batting.

7

Stitch around the outer edges through all the layers using ¹/4" seams, leaving an opening for turning.

8

9

Trim across the corners. Turn the checkerboard right side out and press lightly. Slipstitch the opening closed.

Continued

Pin-baste the layers together with safety pins in the center of the squares, starting from the center and working out to the edges. Set your sewing machine for a zig zag stitch (W-5.0 mm) and a short stitch length (L-0.5 mm). Lower the feed dogs so the fabric won't move forward when stitching. Bartack through all the layers at each corner where the squares meet.

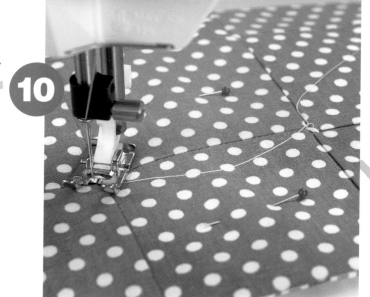

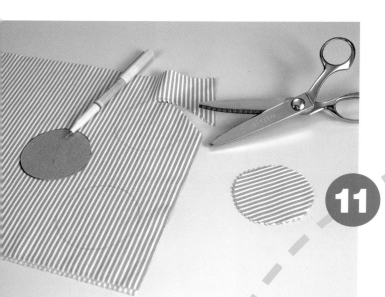

Copy the circle pattern from the CD and trace it onto cardboard. Trace 24 circles each on two contrasting fabrics. Cut out the circles along the marking using your pinking shears.

Place two circles, wrong sides together, and stitch a 1/4" seam, leaving a small opening for filling.

13 Make a funnel from the piece of paper and fill each circle with beans. Stitch the opening closed.

14 Make a carrying bag for your checkerboard and checkers by cutting two 18" x 15" rectangles from the cotton print fabric of your choice. Cut one strip 45" x 2" for the tie.

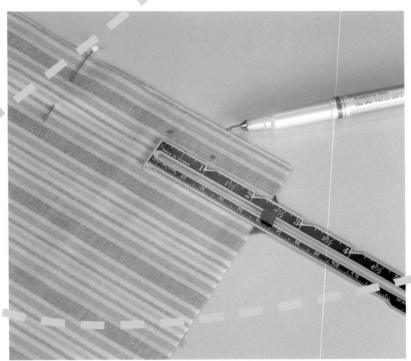

15 On one 18" side of the bag, measure and mark 1 1/4" down from the top edge, and then mark again 1" down from the first mark for the opening for the drawstring.

Continued

 Mark ¹/2" seam allowances along the 18" sides and one 15" side. With right sides together, pin the bag pieces together and begin stitching at the upper edge, leaving an opening between the markings for the drawstring.

Finish the seam allowances by pinking the edges and pressing the seams flat. Trim diagonally across the corners; turn the bag to the right side and press.

17

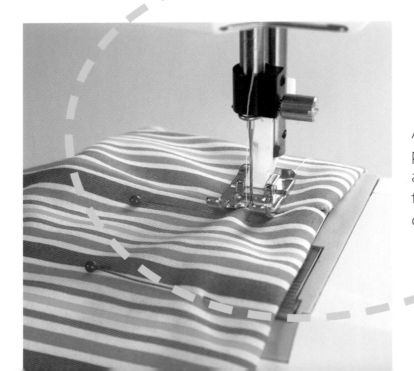

At the open upper edge, press under ¹/4". Press under again 1". Edgestitch close to the pressed edge to make a casing for the drawstring.

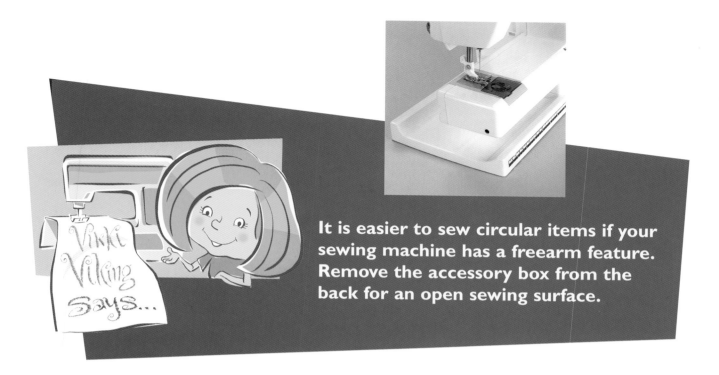

It is easier to sew circular items if your sewing machine has a freearm feature. Remove the accessory box from the back for an open sewing surface.

Vikki Viking Says...

19

To make the drawstring, press under ¹/4" along each long edge and at each end of the strip. Fold the strip in half lengthwise and pin. Edgestitch close to the edges. Using a bodkin or large safety pin attached to the end of the strip, insert the drawstring through the opening at the side of the casing. Tie a knot at each end of the drawstring.

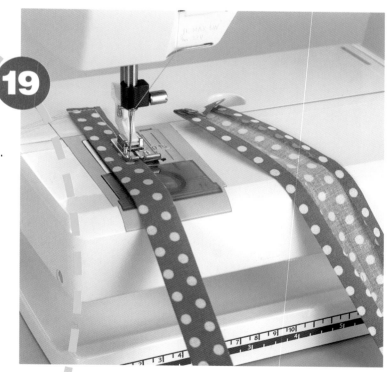

20

Roll up the checkerboard and place it in the bag with the checkers for traveling.

Strip-pieced Place Mats

Learn how to strip piece by making these easy place mats. The perfect gift for Mom and you can decorate them anyway you want! Choose your favorite colors to mix and match.

Gather your supplies:

- ¹/₂ yard each of three or four coordinating cotton print fabrics
- ¹/₂ yard of striped or coordinating cotton print fabric for backing
- ¹/₂ yard of cotton batting
- Baby and Jumbo Rick Rack
- Polyester sewing thread
- Sewing scissors
- Rotary cutter and mat
- Ruler
- Marking pencil, pen, or chalk
- Safety pins
- Glue stick

1 Let's get started:

Print the diagram and pattern from the CD. For four place mats, cut 24 strips, 16¹/₂" × 2¹/₂", from the coordinating prints. Cut four corner squares using the pattern. Cut four backing pieces, 16¹/₂ " × 12¹/₂", and cut four batting pieces the same size.

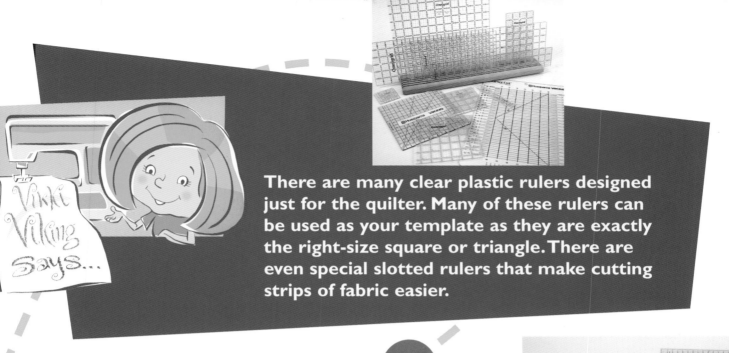

There are many clear plastic rulers designed just for the quilter. Many of these rulers can be used as your template as they are exactly the right-size square or triangle. There are even special slotted rulers that make cutting strips of fabric easier.

Vikki Viking Says...

2

Place six strips face up on your work surface to determine the layout. Cut off 4¹/4" from the top two strips to allow for the corner square.

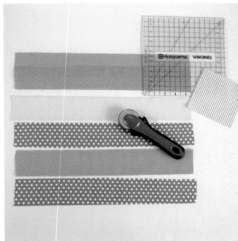

First, with right sides together, stitch the long edges of the two shorter strips using a ¹/4" seam allowance. Press the seam to one side. Stitch the square to the end of the shorter strips. Continue stitching the remaining strips to the long edges.

3

4

As you stitch each strip to the next, press the seams to one side.

Continued

5

Put the batting on your work surface and layer the pieced top right side up over it. Place safety pins about 2"-3" apart to hold the layers together.

Alternate wide and narrow rick rack strips over the seams and keep in place with a glue stick or straight pins. Stitch the rick rack through the center through all the layers.

6

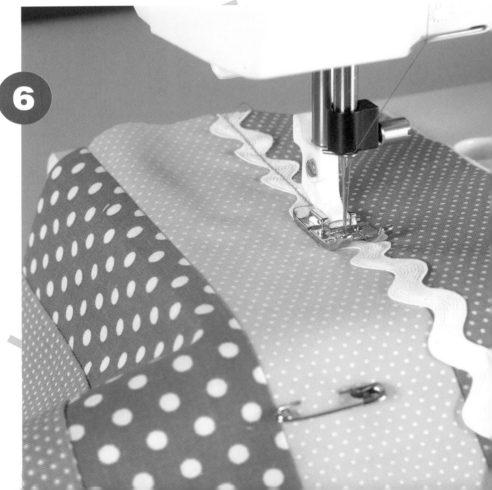

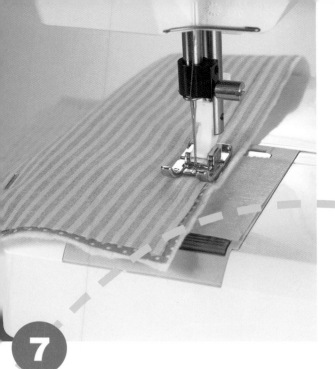

Trim the corners and turn the place mat to the right side; press. Turn in the edges of the fabric and batting at the opening; pin. Edgestitch ¼" from the edge around the place mat on all four sides.

7

Pin the place mat backing to the front with right sides together. Stitch around the edge using a ¼" seam allowance leaving a 4" opening for turning.

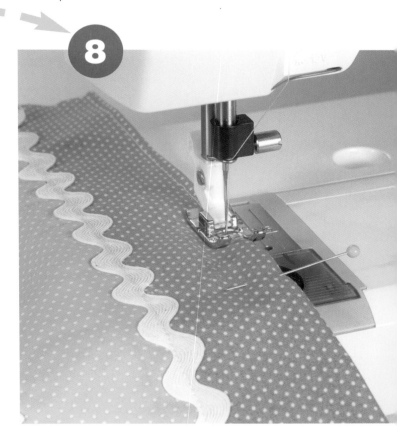

8

Just Sew You Know

Use the edges of your presser foot as your guide when topstitching or try an edge-stitching foot which has a guide attached to help in guiding your fabric. Always watch and guide with the foot rather than the needle for straight sewing!

Soft Pillow with Heart

A soft pillow to hug may be just the thing that a sick child or adult needs for comfort. Extend your heart and make this simple pillow. Donate your project to a local children's hospital or other charitable organization.

Gather your supplies:

- ¹/₂ yard each of red and white fleece
- Red or white felt
- 18" x 22" pillow form
- Fusible webbing
- Pattern tracing material
- Sewing scissors
- Pinking sheers
- Ruler
- Fabric marking pen, pencil, or chalk
- Polyester sewing thread
- Hand-sewing needle

Let's get started:

Copy the rectangle pattern from the CD. Copy the heart pattern from "It's a Heart!" Transfer both to pattern tracing material. Cut one 19" x 23" rectangle from each color of fleece. Using the heart pattern, cut one from either red or white felt.

2 With the pinking sheers, cut around the felt heart.

3

Cut a piece of fusible webbing from the heart pattern. Find the center of the rectangle on the opposite color fleece and, following the manufacturer's instructions, fuse the heart section to the fleece.

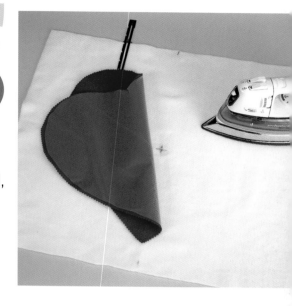

4

With right sides together, pin the pillow front to the back section leaving an opening for turning. Stitch 1/2" from the edges.

Trim across the corners and turn the pillow to the right side. Insert the pillow form and slipstitch the opening closed.

5

Handy Foldaway Blanket

Fold up this soft cover into its own pocket for easy storage. For a homeless child this might be the only possession they can carry away with them, and it's comforting and soft, too!

Gather your supplies:

- $2^1/8$ yards of printed fleece
- 2 yards of solid fleece
- $1^1/8$ yards of $^1/2$"-wide coordinating grosgrain ribbon
- $^5/8$ yard of $1^1/2$"-wide grosgrain ribbon
- Jumbo Rick Rack
- 24 mm snap setting tool
- 6 – 1" buttons
- Polyester sewing thread
- Sewing scissors

Let's get started:

1 Cut one 57" x 72" rectangle from each piece of fleece. Cut one 20" square from the printed fleece for the foldaway pocket. Save a small scrap of the solid fleece for the snap backing.

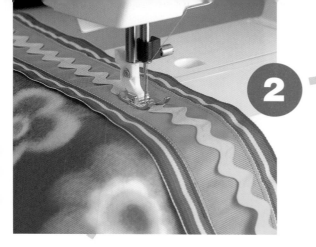

2 Lay the ¹/₂"-wide ribbon along one edge of the pocket and cut the ribbon ¹/₂" longer than the pocket. Pin the ribbon to one edge of the pocket and turn under ¹/₄" at each end. Topstitch along both edges. Following the same procedure, sew a 1¹/₂"-wide grosgrain ribbon next and then add another row of narrow grosgrain ribbon. Center the Jumbo Rick Rack trim over the 1¹/₂" grosgrain ribbon and stitch in place.

Just Sew You Know

A ribbon-trimmed pocket looks great, but it does more than that. Woven ribbons help to add strength to an edge that would otherwise stretch when the fleece blanket is tucked inside. Also, the trims add support for the snap closure.

3 Find the center of the trimmed edge. Following the manufacturer's instructions, apply a cap and socket using a snap setting tool.

4 Find the center of one short side of the solid rectangle. Find the center of the pocket opposite the ribbon-trimmed side. With the ribbon-trimmed side down, pin the pocket over the solid fleece matching the center marks and the cut edges. Sew the pocket to the fleece rectangle, leaving the ribbon-trimmed side open.

Continued

Decorative snaps are a great closure to use on everything from this blanket to a simple vest or jacket. Each set-in snap has four pieces; a cap, a socket and a two-piece prong with ring. Use a snap setting tool to apply.

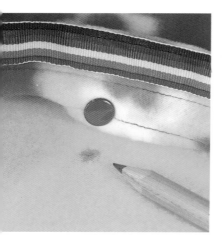

5 Use a fabric marking pencil to make a dot on the fleece rectangle, just underneath the snap on the pocket.

Place a small scrap of fleece behind the dot and, following the manufacturer's instructions, poke the prongs of the snap ring through both layers of fleece. Remove the post of the snap setting tool to set the snap stud.

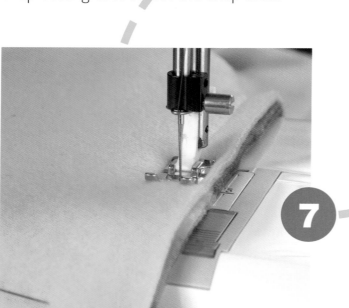

6

7 Pin the edge of the fleece rectangles, right sides together, with the ribbon-trimmed pocket between the layers. Sew all four sides with a 1/2" seam allowance; leave a 12" opening on one side for turning. Trim the corners. Pull the blanket through the opening.

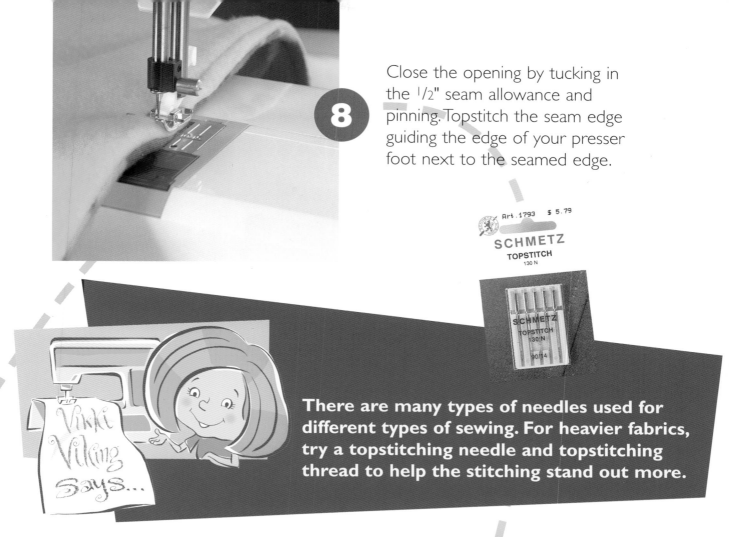

8 Close the opening by tucking in the 1/2" seam allowance and pinning. Topstitch the seam edge guiding the edge of your presser foot next to the seamed edge.

Art.1793 $ 5.79

SCHMETZ
TOPSTITCH
130 N

There are many types of needles used for different types of sewing. For heavier fabrics, try a topstitching needle and topstitching thread to help the stitching stand out more.

Keep the two layers of fleece from shifting by sewing buttons across one side. Lay the throw on a flat surface and mark the placement for three buttons 12" apart and 18" from the finished edge above each side of the pocket. Sew the buttons by machine through both layers of fleece.

9

Neatly fold the blanket so it matches the size of the ribbon-trimmed pocket. Turn the pocket right side out over the folded throw and it's stored, ready to use again!

10

What Size Am I?

ComfortCap™
(page 152)

Bed Cape
(page 148)

What Size

Sewing Exercises—Taking Your Body Measurements

Before you can begin sewing for yourself, you need to figure out what size you are! Taking your body measurements is very important for selecting the correct size of pattern. Although you can take measurements yourself, its best to measure with your mom or an adult to be sure the measurements are accurate. A tape measure is the perfect tool for measuring.

The following measurements are needed to determine your pattern size. Record your numbers on the chart that you copied off the CD. It's the same as the one shown here and you can take it with you to the fabric store to buy your pattern. Check your sizes with the measurements on the pattern envelope and record any differences in the + or – column. It is usually better to select the larger size pattern than the smaller if you need to make an adjustment.

My Body Measurements

For Girls:	My measurement	+ or - Adjustment	Pattern Size
A. Chest			
B. Bust			
C. Waist			
D. Hips			
For Boys:			
A. Neckband			
B. Chest			
C. Waist			
D. Shirt Sleeve Length			
E. Hips			

Am I?

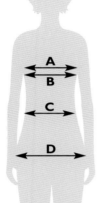

For Girls:

Begin by tying a string around your waist then bend from side to side so the string will be at your natural waistline. Now stand comfortably and look straight ahead.

A. Chest—measure around your body under the arms and above the bust.

B. Bust—measure around the fullest part of your bust. Be sure the tape measure is straight across the fullest part of your back.

C. Waist—measure around your natural waistline, over the string.

D. Hips—measure around the fullest part of your hips, about 7" down from your natural waistline.

For Boys:

A. Neckband—measure around the fullest part of your neck and add ¹/2".

B. Chest—measure around the fullest part of your chest.

C. Waist—tie a string around the area of your waist that is most comfortable for you OR where you usually wear your pants. Measure around the waistline over the string.

D. Shirt Sleeve Length—bend the arm up at the elbow. Measure from the base of the neck, along the back and arm to the elbow then up to the wrist.

E. Hips—measure around the fullest part of your hips, about 7" down from your natural waistline.

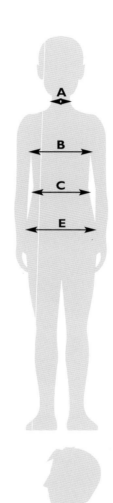

Working with Patterns

There are lots of patterns in the catalogs you see at the fabric store, and it can be confusing and scary trying to decide which one to buy. Take your time and study the designs as you make up your mind. It is important to understand what information is on the pattern envelope and how to read the instruction sheet found inside the envelope before you purchase a pattern. A little bit of information will ensure that you buy the right-size pattern each time. Watch the videos on the CD to learn more!

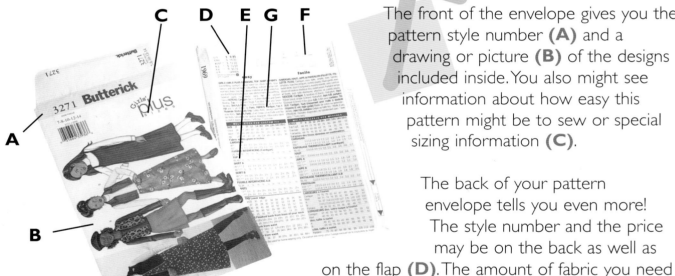

The front of the envelope gives you the pattern style number **(A)** and a drawing or picture **(B)** of the designs included inside. You also might see information about how easy this pattern might be to sew or special sizing information **(C)**.

The back of your pattern envelope tells you even more! The style number and the price may be on the back as well as on the flap **(D)**. The amount of fabric you need for your size **(E)** and the specific garment you have selected is shown **(F)**. A description of the garment, fabrics that are best suited for this project, and any notions you need (buttons, zippers, trim, etc.) are listed **(G)**.

The pattern instruction sheet provides you with lots of help. It shows what the front and back of the garment looks like **(A)** and a drawing of each pattern piece with the name of each piece **(B)**. A fabric-cutting layout for your size and the view of the pattern you are making is given to help you lay out the pattern pieces correctly on the right width fabric **(C)**. And there

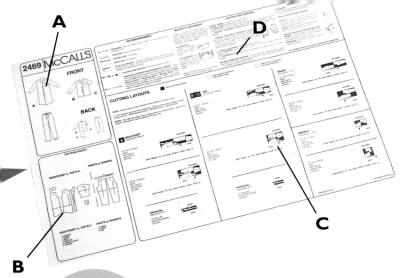

usually is general information about symbols, cutting and marking, and sewing information used in the pattern **(D)** on this sheet.

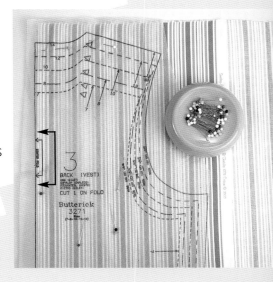

Once you have chosen your pattern, select the correct pieces for the view you are making. Read all the information printed on the front of the pattern pieces before pinning. Pin any fabric pieces marked "place on fold" along the lengthwise folded edge of the fabric. The straight edge of the pattern should be even with the fold.

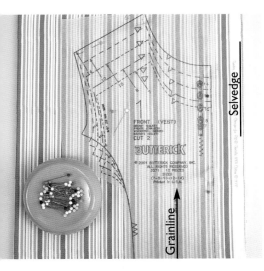

Pin all the pattern pieces in place according to the pattern layout on your instruction sheet. The lengthwise grainline shown on the pattern piece should be parallel to the selvedge of your fabric.

Cut out your pattern along the solid cutting line. If your pattern is multi-size, cut along the lines for your size. When you reach a notch, carefully clip around the notch with the tip of your scissors, then continue cutting along the solid line.

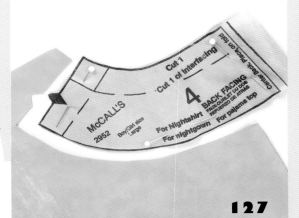

Important Sewing Terms and Techniques

There are a few special techniques you will use when sewing garments. There is more information on the video on the CD to help you.

Fusing

Some of your projects may require interfacing. Following the manufacturer's instructions, place your fabric pattern piece right side down on your ironing board. Next, place the interfacing glue or shiny side down on the wrong side of your pattern piece. Cover the entire piece with a dampened press cloth and press the interfacing to the pattern piece.

Sewing a Blindhem

Speed up your sewing by learning to hem by machine. To sew a blindhem, set your sewing machine to a blindhem stitch and attach a blindhem foot. Measure, turn up, and press the hem to the wrong side of your garment. Then flip the hem back to the right side. Stitch so the folded edge of the fabric rests against the right inside edge of the presser foot and the zig zag stitch just pierces the fold of the fabric.

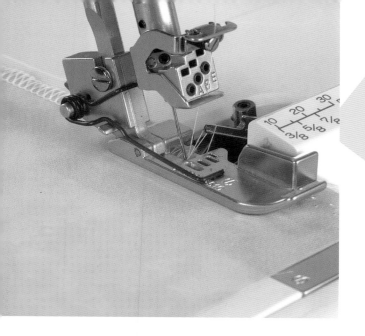

Overcasting

Overcast the fabric with a serger or overlock machine for a clean-finished edge. Using one needle and three threads, place the edge of the fabric even with the edge of the presser foot and sew. Watch the video on the CD for more information about the serger. Other serger stitches are also shown.

Topstitching

For precise topstitching, place the finished edge of your project against the inside edge of the blindhem foot, as shown here, or against the center guide on an edge-joining foot. Move your needle so the stitches are the exact distance you want them from the edge of your fabric.

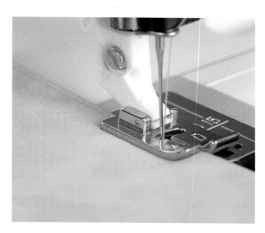

Sewing Trims

Use the toes on your blindhem foot as a guide when sewing on trim. Place the edge of the trim along the inside edge of the right toe and adjust your needle position so it stitches close to the edge of your trim.

Sleepytime Nightshirt or PJ's

Choose a fun, flannel print and sew up a cozy nightshirt or pajama pants for yourself. Perfect for sleepovers or just snuggling with a good book in your own bed!

Gather your supplies:

- Nightshirt or pajama pattern of choice (such as McCall's #2952 or #2469)
- Flannel fabric - see pattern envelope for yardage requirements
- Fusible interfacing - see pattern envelope for yardage requirements
- Polyester sewing thread
- Fabric marking pencil, pen, or chalk
- Seam gauge
- Sewing scissors
- Pins
- Large safety pin or bodkin
- Buttons or elastic according to pattern

We suggest that you learn to read and follow the pattern sewing directions provided with each pattern. It is important that you understand what the directions are telling you to do. Rather than duplicate the pattern directions here, we are showing you special techniques or sections of the construction that may be a little confusing or more difficult to understand.

Let's get started:

1. Following the suggested layout, cut out the nightshirt or pajama pants pattern in your size. If you have chosen a fabric that has nap or a one-way design be sure to use the layout "with nap."

Nap means your fabric has a surface texture that does not look the same from all directions. If you run your hand across the fabric in different directions, you'll feel the texture and see shading. Flannel and corduroy are fabrics with a nap.

Begin reading and following the steps in the sewing directions. We are going to follow a flat construction process in sewing the nightshirt. A fusible interfacing will work well on the facing of the nightshirt. Remember to use a press cloth when fusing.

2

Vikki Viking Says...

One method of finishing the edges of the facing is to turn the edge under 1/4" and stitch in place. By finishing the edge, you keep the fabric from raveling and fraying.

3

Once the facing has been attached to the neckline, trim and clip the seams before turning to the right side. Turn and press. Topstitch the facing 1" from the edge using your quilt guide to keep the stitching straight.

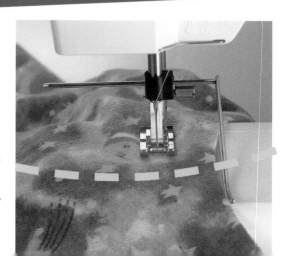

Continued

131

4 Before you sew the side seams, sew in the sleeves by using the flat method. Pin the sleeve to the shoulder and armhole matching all the marks and notches. Sew. Once the sleeves are sewn in, sew the side and sleeve seams at one time. Clip the seams as necessary.

5

For a very flat seam finish once the seams are sewn, overcast the seams with the serger or an overcast stitch on your sewing machine for a neat finish. Your project will last longer and look better because the threads cover the edge.

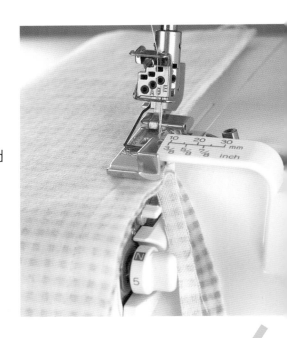

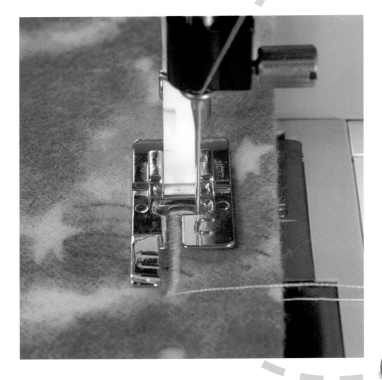

Always sew out a sample buttonhole first using the same fabric as your garment. Some machines stitch forward first and some stitch backwards for the first side so be sure to check your presser foot position. Using the buttonhole foot with your machine, stitch the exact-size buttonholes on the front.

6

Using the marks on the pattern tissue as a guide only, mark the placement for the buttons on the nightshirt. Measure the width of your buttons then measure the depth. Add 1/4" and use this number as the length of your buttonhole. Mark the placement of the buttonholes evenly apart.

7

Just Sew You Know

On some of today's sewing machines, a special foot is available that sews the same size buttonholes over and over for you. This sensor buttonhole foot "tells" the sewing machine computer the right-size buttonhole to make when you tell it the size of button you are using.

8

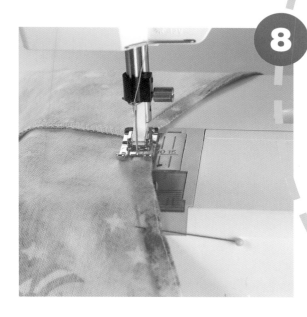

An easy way to make sure your double-turned hems are even is first, sew a line of stitches 5/8" from the raw edge. Turn the hem up to the stitching line and press. Turn the raw edge into the fold and press again for a double-fold hem. Stitch close to the inside turned edge.

9

For the pajama pants, begin by following the sewing directions with the pattern. Each inside leg seam is sewn first.

Continued

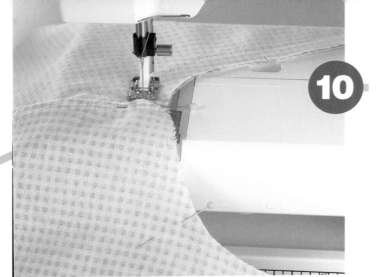

10 Match the inside leg seams and sew the center seam using the reinforced straight stitch on your machine. The reinforced straight stitch is the best stitch to use in high stress areas because the stitch gets sewn three times. Stitch the front to the back at the sides.

Vikki Viking Says...

Other seam finishes that can be used are the 3-step zig zag sewn on the edge of each seam allowance or a 3-thread serger stitch sewing and trimming the seam allowances at the same time.

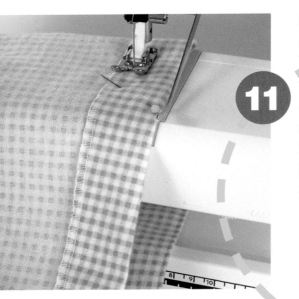

11 Finish the upper edge with one of the seam finishes. Turn down the upper edge for the elastic waistband casing following the markings on the pattern. Stitch the casing in place leaving a 3" opening to insert the elastic.

Using a large safety pin or bodkin, thread the elastic through the casing.

12

Overlap the ends of the elastic and pin. Draw a small square on the elastic for your stitching line. Follow the line and stitch the ends of the elastic together. Stitch the opening closed.

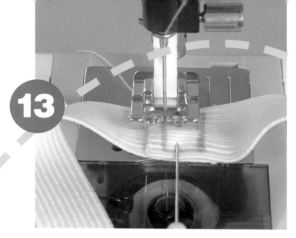

13

To keep the elastic from shifting in the casing, use your edge-joining foot to "stitch-in-the-ditch" through the casing and the elastic at the seam line.

14

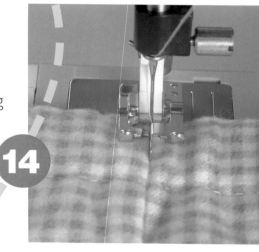

Just Sew You Know

"Stitch-in-the-ditch" is a term used when sewing into a seamline. This technique can be used to hold elastic in place, keep facings from rolling out, and attaching binding to edges. The edge-joining foot has a center bar that makes sewing exactly into the seam easier.

Try your pants on to measure the exact length. Trim the hem to 1 1/4" deep when folded up. Finish the raw edge with one of the seam finishes shown above and then stitch each pant leg hem in place.

15

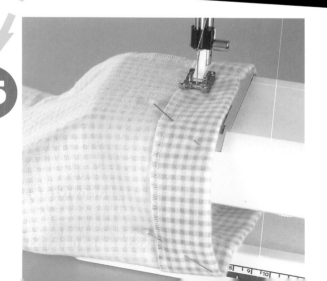

Easy-to-Make Skirt

A skirt is an easy way to begin sewing for yourself. Multi-size and plus-size patterns offer you a lot of options. Make one or many and then add a vest or jumper, too!

Gather your supplies:

- Skirt pattern of choice (such as Butterick #3271 or #6961)
- Fabric - see pattern envelope for fabric suggestions and yardage requirements
- Fusible interfacing - see pattern envelope for yardage requirements
- $1/2$"-wide elastic
- Polyester sewing thread
- Sewing scissors
- Pinking shears
- Marking pencil, pen, or chalk
- Pins
- Seam gauge
- Large safety pin or bodkin

1 Let's get started:

Layout your pattern pieces according to the layout chart on the sewing directions sheet. To allow for growth in height, add a $2^{1}/2$" hem to the pattern. First check how much hem allowance has already been added to the pattern. This pattern has a $5/8$" hem allowance. Just add 2" to the bottom of your pattern for a generous $2^{1}/2$" hem. Cut out all pieces from the fabric and interfacing. Transfer all the important marks from the pattern to your fabric.

Just Sew You Know

Since the pattern we chose is multi-size, you may want to keep the other sizes on the pattern for future use. Simply trace your exact size onto pattern tracing material and you can use the original pattern tissues over and over again.

One way to extend the life of your garment, especially when you are still growing, is to add a generous hem allowance. A common hem allowance is 2-2½". A wider hem helps the garment grow with you! You can add a hem allowance to the pattern by drawing a line on your pattern 2" below the cutting line. Or trace the pattern onto pattern tracing material and add the new hem allowance. This will help eliminate confusion between different sizes on the pattern when you start cutting out the pieces.

Following the manufacturer's instructions, fuse the interfacing to the wrong side of the front facing.

2

Continued

3

Overcast the edge of the front facing for a flatter edge. You can use a serger or an overcast stitch on your sewing machine. With right sides together, stitch the facing to the skirt front following the pattern instructions.

Pink the facing seam allowances before turning the facing to the right side. The pinked edge will allow your seam to lay flatter.

4

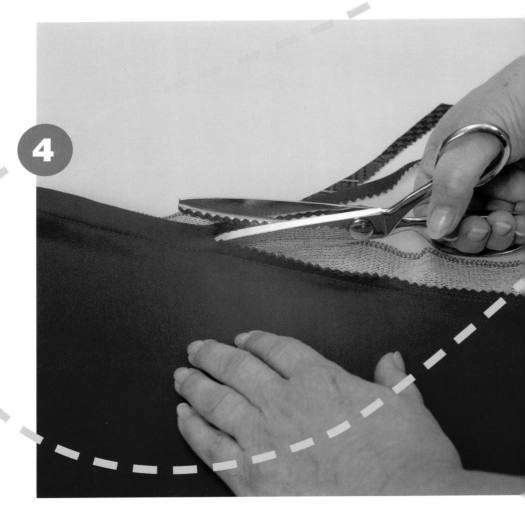

5 Understitch the facing before turning the facing to the inside. "Understitching" is done by sewing very close to the seam through the facing and the seam allowance to keep the facing from rolling out when you wear the garment. Using an edge-joining foot, place the guide in the seam and move the needle to the side for stitching.

6 Before turning down the edge for the elastic casing on the skirt back, clean-finish the top edge and sides of the skirt back piece. A 3-step zig zag is another option for an edge finish.

7 Turn down the casing and stitch in place.

Continued

8

Check the sewing directions chart for the length of elastic to cut for your size. Use a large safety pin or a bodkin to thread the elastic through the casing. Keep the elastic ends even with the side raw edges.

Pin the front section to the back according to the directions. Stitch the side seams through all the layers.

9

10

Try on your skirt to make sure the length is correct. Using a seam gauge, turn up a 2¹/₂" hem; pin in place. Select a blindhem stitch on your sewing machine and attach the blindhem foot. Fold the hem back on itself (it should look like a backward "S") so the finished edge of your skirt is extending about ¹/₄" beyond the fold of the skirt. Adjust the zig zag portion of the stitch so it just catches the fold of the skirt.

If you need to lengthen your skirt and the old hemline shows once you've adjusted the hem allowance, add a ribbon trim to the outside. A narrow ¹/₄"-¹/₂" ribbon can easily be sewn with a zig zag stitch over the old hemline.

Vikki Viking Says...

A Chef's Apron for the Barbecue "King or Queen"

Barbecuing can be a family affair! What a great gift for Mom and Dad, and then make one of these great aprons for yourself, too! Embroider a name or decorate the aprons any way you desire.

Gather your supplies:

- Barbecue apron Pattern of choice (such as Butterick #4119)
- Fabric - see pattern envelope for fabric suggestions and yardage requirements
- 2¹/₂ yards of cotton webbing or strapping
- ¹/₃ yard of contrasting fabric for optional pocket
- 2 D-rings
- Polyester sewing thread
- Sewing scissors
- Fabric marking pencil, pen, or chalk
- Pins
- Ruler
- Fast-turn™ tube turning tool (optional)

Let's get started:

1

Follow the pattern layout directions for cutting out the apron. Add a pocket to the front by cutting one 11" × 13¹/₂" rectangle from contrasting fabric. Use the tie pattern to cut two ties from the webbing. From the remaining webbing, cut one 23¹/₂"-long piece and one 5"-long piece. Transfer all the markings to the fabric from the pattern tissue.

Just Sew You Know

For strong seams that last, backstitch at the start and finish of each seam. Begin each seam by taking 2-3 stitches forward, then backstitch 2-3 stitches and continue your seam. Finish the seam by stitching to the end of the fabric, then backstitch 2-3 stitches and then sew forward to the end of the fabric.

To one of the long sides of the pocket, sew 1" from the edge. Press the edge to the wrong side along the stitching line. Then, press the cut edge into the fold to make a 1/2" double-fold hem. Sew along the inside folded edge of the pocket. Sew, using a very long stitch length, 1/2" from the edge along the other three sides. Press the edges along the stitching lines to the wrong side.

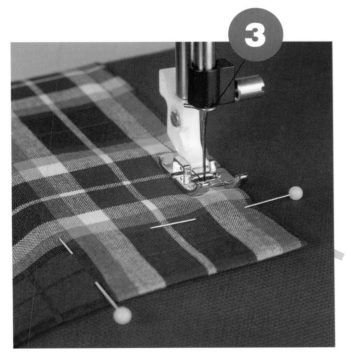

Fold the short edges of the pocket together; mark the center. Fold the sides of the apron together and crease to mark the center. Measure and pin the hemmed edge of the pocket 13" from the top of the apron, lining up the mark on the pocket with the apron crease. Using the edge of your presser foot or an edge stitching foot as a guide, topstitch along three sides of the pocket.

Continued

4

Using the center crease as your guide for stitching, sew through the center of the pocket to make two sections.

Before you sew the apron together, decorate the front with embroidery or other methods of decoration. If you have an embroidery machine, stitching designs or letters is as easy as inserting a disc and threading your machine!

5

Finish one end of each of the three long ties. Fold 1/4" over, then fold the end over again so the cut edge of the tie is enclosed. Sew close to the inside folded edge of the tie. Pin the ties to the sides at the appropriate marks.

6

Thread the small piece of strapping through the D-rings. Fold the strapping in half and pin to the right side of the upper-right hand corner of the apron. Sew the strap in place. Sew one end of the remaining webbing to the upper left corner.

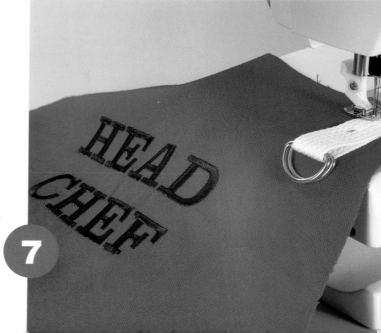

7

8 Lengthen your sewing machine stitch to a basting stitch. Stitch around the outside edge of the apron 5/8" from the raw edge.

Trim across the corners of the apron. Press the edge to the wrong side at the stitching line, then press the cut edge into the fold, creating a miter at each corner and a double-fold hem around the edge. Sew along the inside folded edge of the apron. Pull out the basting stitch. **9**

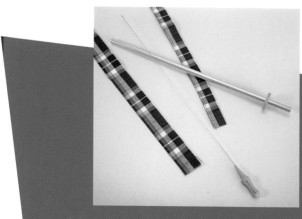

Vikki Viking Says...

Make ties from your contrasting fabric instead of using cotton webbing. Follow the pattern directions for sewing. On the sewn end, trim the seam allowance. Use a Fast-turn™ tube turner, to quickly turn the straps to the right side. Press the ties and finish with topstitching.

Terry Cloth Wrap for Mom

This easy sewing project is a wonderful way to surprise Mom on her next birthday or Christmas. She'll be so proud that you made it yourself!

Gather your supplies:

- Terry wrap pattern of choice (such as Butterick pattern #5027)
- Terry-cloth or cotton chenille fabric - see pattern envelope for yardage requirements
- Crocheted lace - see pattern envelope for yardage requirements
- Jumbo Rick Rack
- Elastic
- Sewing scissors
- Polyester sewing thread
- Fabric marking pencil, pen or chalk
- Pins

Let's get started:

Cut out your pattern according to the layout directions. Mark and pin the crocheted lace following the pattern directions. Stitch in place. Sew the facing strip to the front.

1

Just Sew You Know

Terry cloth and cotton chenille are heavy fabrics. Be sure to use a heavier needle (size #90/14) and lengthen your stitch to easily sew through the fabric.

Place the rick rack over the crocheted lace and the facing seam. Stitch down the center of the rick rack through all the layers.

2

3

Finish the raw edges with a serged or overcast stitch. It will be flatter and less bulky when the casing is turned down.

4

Continue following the pattern directions to complete the wrap. Turn the facing in at the side and catch the edge with your blindhem stitch.

Terry cloth fabric ravels very easily. After sewing traditional seams, press open the seams and stitch the edges down using the 3-step zig zag. Even though the stitching will go through to the right side, the fabric is "loopy" and the stitching will be hidden but your seams will be stronger and won't ravel.

A Cozy Bed Cape

Most patterns can be used in a variety of ways. Use this evening wrap pattern to make a special fleece bed wrap for someone confined to their bed. It's warm, cozy, and fun to make.

Gather your supplies:

- Cape pattern of choice (such as McCall's #3033)
- Fleece fabric - see pattern envelope for yardage requirements
- Flat lace and decorative trim - see pattern envelope for yardage requirements
- 1¾ yards of 1"-wide grosgrain ribbon for neckline trim and ties
- Sewing scissors
- Polyester sewing thread
- Pins

Let's get started:

1 Pin and cut out your pattern according to the appropriate pattern layout. Do not cut a neck facing; it will be substituted with a grosgrain-ribbon neck finish.

2 Sew the center back pieces together with right sides together. Trim away half of one seam allowance.

Open out the back section, turn the wide seam allowance over the trimmed seam allowance, and pin from the right side. Place your presser foot over the seam allowances, next to the seamline, and topstitch the seam in place.

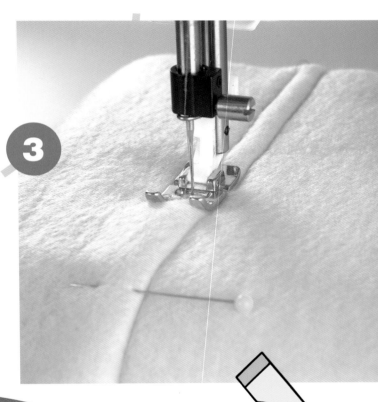

3

Just Sew You Know

There are many different types of seams you can use on your garments. A seam folded to one side and topstitched is called a "welt" seam. Learn how to sew all the other seam types.

Continued

4

Sew the front cape pieces to the back. Repeat the seam treatment in Step 3. Pin the trim 3^1/$_2$" away from the bottom edge. Use a seam gauge to help keep the trim even. Use a stitch that is appropriate to hold your trim in place.

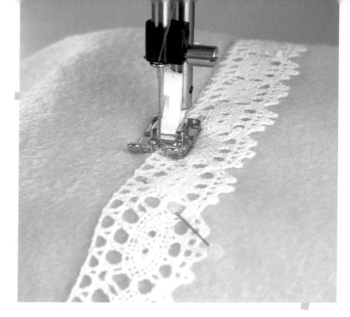

Sew rosette trim to the edge of the flat lace with a straight stitch.

5

Set your straight stitch to the longest stitch length for basting and sew ^{5}/$_8$" from the front and hem edge of the cape. Using the stitching line as a guide, turn the fleece toward the inside of the cape. Trim the corners and sew the edges placing the edge of your presser foot along the fold of the hem.

6

Fold the 1"-wide ribbon in half and mark the center. Lay the neck facing pattern piece over the ribbon and match the center of the pattern with the center fold in the ribbon. Transfer the marks from the pattern piece onto the ribbon to indicate the front neck edge of the cape.

7

8 Finger-crease the ribbon in half lengthwise. Place the pattern piece back over the creased portion of the ribbon. Use a fabric marker to transfer lines indicating the front edge, shoulder seam, and center back of neck.

Encase the neckline of the cape with the creased ribbon. Match the marks on the ribbon with the front edges, the shoulder seams, and the center back seam; pin. Topstitch close to the edge of the ribbon, sewing from the front edge of the cape around the neckline. Trim the ends of the ribbon at an angle to prevent raveling.

9

Vikki Viking Says...

Choose a pattern that offers many different views or a number of projects in one envelope. You are getting a lot more choices for your money. Enjoy making all the pieces shown from many different fabrics.

ComfortCap™

It is truly a wonderful thing to contribute your time or talents. Cancer patients face many physical challenges most often due to the medical treatment they are enduring. Sew up this soft hat out of a pretty 100% cotton knit to show you care.

Gather your supplies:

- Adult - $1/2$ yard of knit or $3/4$ yard of woven fabric
- Child - $1/3$ yard of knit or $5/8$ yard of woven fabric
- Clear elastic
- Polyester sewing thread
- Sewing scissors
- Pinking shears
- Fabric marking pencil, pen, or chalk
- Pattern tracing material
- Pins

Let's get started:

1 Copy the adult or child's cap pattern from the CD. Trace the pattern onto the pattern tracing material and transfer all the markings. Be sure to choose the correct seam allowance for the size of the patient's head.

Just Sew You Know

Measure around the head just above the eyebrows and ears remembering the size may change after hair loss. Adjust the size by making larger or smaller seam allowances.

2

Place the pattern on the fabric using the "stretch" line as your guide across the stretchiest part of your fabric. Cut two pieces, one for the cap and one for the lining. Transfer all the markings to the fabric.

Sew the outside darts first starting at the edge and sewing to the dot. The darts give the hat its shape.

3

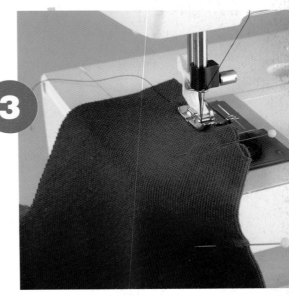

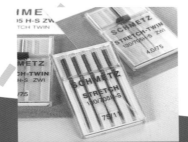

If you are sewing on a lightweight knit fabric, be sure to use a stretch needle in a standard size of #75/11. The slightly rounded point on the needle will keep the fabric from running. Heavy knits may require a size #90/14.

Also, if possible, reduce the presser foot pressure on your machine to prevent rippling when sewing on knits.

Vikki Viking Says...

Continued

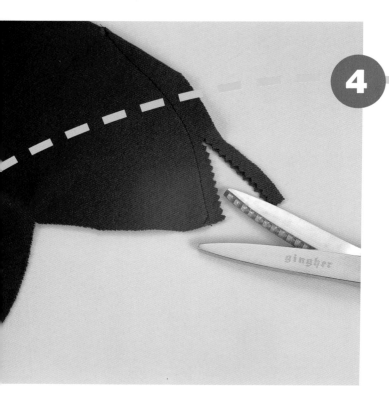

4 Trim the seams with your pinking shears to reduce any bulk.

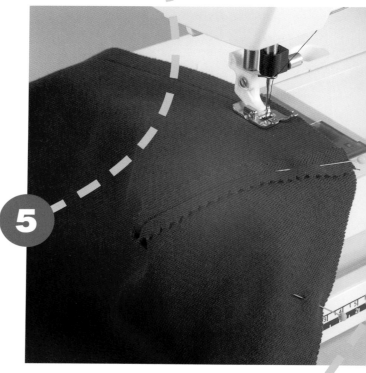

5 Sew the center back seam and into the center dart to the dot. Trim the seam allowances and finger-press the seams open. Repeat steps 3 through 5 for the lining.

Just Sew You Know

A dart looks like a triangle on a pattern and gives fullness and dimension to the garment. To sew a dart, the long lines of the triangle are brought together and the dart is sewn from the wide to the narrow point.

Place the two hats inside each other, right sides together, matching the seam lines and center fronts. Match the brim edges and pin. To prevent the brim of the cap from rippling after much washing and wearing, support the brim seam with clear elastic. Pin the elastic around the brim of the cap, centering it over the seamline. Stitch around the edge through the elastic using the correct seam allowance. Do not pull the elastic when sewing. Leave a 3" opening for turning.

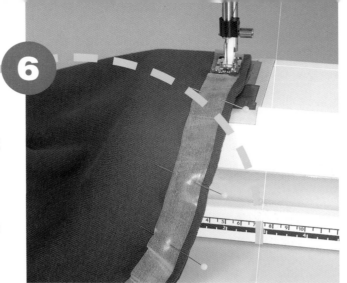

6

Just Sew You Know

Elastic used for support helps seams "remember" their original length and shape. The addition of clear elastic helps the stretched seams spring back. The clear elastic is softer and more pliable than woven elastic, therefore perfect for this project.

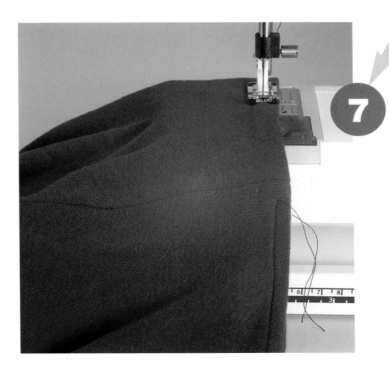

7

Turn the hat to the right side and turn the open edge in. Topstitch around the edge placing your presser foot along the edge of the fabric.

Index

Acknowledgements

We gratefully acknowledge the following companies for their support and the contribution of their products toward the production of this book. We hope you continue to support these companies by purchasing their products at your local sewing machine dealer and fabric store. Remember to Keep the World Sewing!

Batting & Pillow Forms
Fairfield Processing Company

Fabrics
Dan River Inc.
P & B Textiles
David Textiles

Felt
National Nonwovens

Ribbon
Offray Ribbon

Threads
Coats & Clark

Stamps & Supplies
Rubber Stampede

Buttons
JHB International

Hook & Loop Tape
Velcro® USA Inc.

Rulers (Safety Shield)
O'LIPFA

Sewing Machines
Husqvarna Viking

Sewing Notions & Quilting Supplies
Prym Dritz Corporation-Omnigrid®

Index

Index

Index

METRIC EQUIVALENTS

Inches to Millimeters and Centimeters
MM - millimeters   CM - centimeters

Inches	MM	CM	Inches	CM	Inches	CM
1/8	3	0.3	9	22.9	30	76.2
1/4	6	0.6	10	25.4	31	78.7
3/8	10	1.0	11	27.9	32	81.3
1/2	13	1.3	12	30.5	33	83.8
5/8	16	1.6	13	33.0	34	86.4
3/4	19	1.9	14	35.6	35	88.9
7/8	22	2.2	15	38.1	36	91.4
1	25	2.5	16	40.6	37	94.0
1 1/4	32	3.2	17	43.2	38	96.5
1 1/2	38	3.8	18	45.7	39	99.1
1 3/4	44	4.4	19	48.3	40	101.6
2	51	5.1	20	50.8	41	104.1
2 1/2	64	6.4	21	53.3	42	106.7
3	76	7.6	22	55.9	43	109.2
3 1/2	89	8.9	23	58.4	44	111.8
4	102	10.2	24	61.0	45	114.3
4 1/2	114	11.4	25	63.5	46	116.8
5	127	12.7	26	66.0	47	119.4
6	152	15.2	27	68.6	48	121.9
7	178	17.8	28	71.1	49	124.5
8	203	20.3	29	73.7	50	127.0

METRIC CONVERSION CHART

Yards	Inches	Meters	Yards	Inches	Meters
1/8	4.5	0.11	1 1/8	40.5	1.03
1/4	9	0.23	1 1/4	45	1.14
3/8	13.5	0.34	1 3/8	49.5	1.26
1/2	18	0.46	1 1/2	54	1.37
5/8	22.5	0.57	1 5/8	58.5	1.49
3/4	27	0.69	1 3/4	63	1.60
7/8	31.5	0.80	1 7/8	67.5	1.71
1	36	0.91	2	72	1.83